NORFC
BROADS

THE BIOGRAPHY

C000235558

NORFOLK BROADS

THE BIOGRAPHY

PETE GOODRUM

For Katie and Ben

Cover illustrations: Both courtesy of the Broads Authority.

First published 2014

Amberley Publishing
The Hill, Stroud
Gloucestershire, GL5 4EP

www.amberley-books.com

Copyright © Pete Goodrum, 2014

The right of Pete Goodrum to be identified as the Author
of this work has been asserted in accordance with the
Copyrights, Designs and Patents Act 1988.

All rights reserved. No part of this book may be reprinted
or reproduced or utilised in any form or by any electronic,
mechanical or other means, now known or hereafter invented,
including photocopying and recording, or in any information
storage or retrieval system, without the permission in writing
from the Publishers.

British Library Cataloguing in Publication Data.
A catalogue record for this book is available from the British Library.

ISBN 978 1 4456 1319 2 (paperback)
ISBN 978 1 4456 1328 4 (ebook)

Typesetting and Origination by Amberley Publishing.
Printed in the UK.

Contents

Acknowledgements

In writing this book I have drawn on the vast amount of material available in books, magazines, research data and reports both in printed form and online. The sheer volume of data available is testament to the enduring interest in the Broads, and I thank each and every one of the writers and scientists, artists and researchers whose work I have studied.

During the writing of the book I have met some of the most interesting, and interested, people I've ever encountered. I have been amazed at their help and co-operation in furnishing me with information, material and pictures. All of them I thank, but there are some to whom I must pay a special acknowledgement.

My very good friend Keith Fox who, when this project was in its infancy, loaned me literally priceless personal material. Thanks Keith.

At Hoseasons, special thanks are due to Simon Altham, Katie Hanger, Geri Colt, Sara West, Rebecca Harris and Mark Chambers. Thank you all for your time, help and enthusiasm.

I'm grateful to Amanda Bunn at Shorthose Russell who kindly helped with valuable introductions.

At the Broads Authority, Hilary Franzen and Bruce Hanson were immensely helpful with their time and resources. Thank you both.

Colin and Lesley Dye at Silvermarine in Brundall were wonderful in talking to me and letting me have access to their archives. We had been neighbours many years earlier and to meet them again on this project was a lovely bonus. Thank you Mr and Mrs Dye.

Sue Bell and Bryan Cadamy, from Summercraft in Hoveton, were a great help in relating their experiences in the boating holiday business. Thank you.

Barbara Greasley and her team, Broads Tours, in Wroxham helped me enormously with insightful conversations and a more-than-useful, and enjoyable, tour of their yard.

I have credited all the photographs to those who helped and supplied them. Thank you. I have made every effort to track down the origins of material and in some cases it has proved impossible. If I have unwittingly reproduced something that you believe to be your property it has been done with the best of intentions and no attempt to avoid crediting you.

To Nicola Gale and the Amberley team I express my thanks for their help and guidance in putting this book together.

And, as ever, huge thanks to my wife Sue. Her constant support is what makes this work possible. Thanks Sue.

Introduction

The Norfolk and Suffolk Broads, to give them their full title, are Britain's largest protected wetland; they are in fact the country's third-largest inland waterway, and they have the status of a national park.

As a 'biography' of the Norfolk Broads, this book sets out to cover many aspects of the region. Such is the richness of the region's history, geography, natural resources, politics and people, it would be possible to write a complete book on any one of those specific topics. Indeed, the Broads have fuelled a rich crop of fictional, and factual, literature. Much of the writing about the area is concerned with, and succeeds in, showing the reader around. For over a century, writers have contributed to a wonderful canon of literature that explains the geography of the Broads, and the towns and villages that make up the landscape.

My purpose became clear in early planning discussions with the ever helpful Nicola Gale at Amberley Publishing. This book was to be a 'history of' rather than a 'guide to' the Broads. Therefore, as far as possible, I have put the story of the Broads into chronological order, with one or two twists and turns where it's been necessary to give some context to a particular point.

The story of the Broads begins with a bleak landscape, in to which man arrived early.

The relationship between humankind and the Broads has been a complex one. An empty expanse became a working environment for peat diggers, who in turn gave way to marsh men, before the Broads became a place of recreation. From that moment the delicate balance between conservation and commerce came precariously into being.

It is an equilibrium that defies a final judgement. Man has made his impact on the Broads, but nature too has held sway. Social and political changes have affected the natural environment, but forces greater than man have taken their toll too. And indeed mankind has contributed to the protection of the environment as well as working there for his profit.

As much as the farmers and fishermen, reed cutters and millwrights, boatbuilders and thatchers all thought they knew the region, the Broads kept something to themselves for almost 1,000 years. It was halfway through the twentieth century before they reminded us of the truth. They were man-made.

This, then, is the story, the biography, of the Norfolk Broads. It's a story of a unique place, where people are proud to do things differently and where the world wants to visit. And so they should. There really is nowhere quite like the Norfolk Broads.

The Biggest Question of All: What Are the Norfolk and Suffolk Broads?

The Broads can best be described as the area of largely navigable broads, lakes, dykes and rivers that, although they spread through Norfolk and Suffolk, are usually known as 'the Norfolk Broads'.

The word 'broad' is often used in talking about the dialect of the county; 'Broad Norfolk' is a familiar term, and plainly describes the strength of the accent. The same adjective is used elsewhere, for example in 'Broad Yorkshire'.

'Broad' as a noun, though, is unusual. It is always dangerous to describe something as unique, but there appear to be no 'broads' other than the 'the Norfolk Broads'. Ranworth Broad is mentioned as early as 1275, but it is nineteenth-century writings that give us some clue as to the meaning or derivation of the term.

In his 1830 publication *The Vocabulary of East Anglia*, Robert Forby's definition for 'Broad' is

> a lake formed by the expansion of a river in a flat country; as Braydon Broad, between Norwich and Yarmouth, and several others in that part of the county of Norfolk; Oulton Broad, & c. in the hundred of Lothingland, in Suffolk.

The 1834 edition of G. Christopher Davies' *Norfolk Broads and Rivers* goes further in relating the Broads to Norfolk specifically, and says,

> The term Broad is peculiar to Norfolk. Its etymology is obvious namely, a broadening out of the rivers into lakes, the Broads being intimately connected with the rivers, which in some cases flow through them, and in others are only divided from them by a reed-bed.
>
> Whittlesea Mere and other parts of the Fen district were the counterparts of the Broads in many respects; but the character of the Fens has so much changed since their drainage, that it is to Norfolk only that one can now look for the wildness and solitude of marsh and mere so dear to the naturalist and sportsman.

By 1987, the lexicographers were rather more to the point. *Chambers Concise Dictionary* of that year makes no mention of 'Broad' under the word Norfolk, although, apart from the county itself, the Norfolk jacket is mentioned. Deep in the definitions of 'broad', which understandably is first dealt with as an adjective, the use as a noun is explained as 'the broad part: (in East Anglia) a lake-like expansion of a river'.

A 2013 visit to Dictionary.com reveals the less than appealing definition of

Broads [brawdz]
noun (used with a plural verb) a low-lying region in E England, in
Norfolk and Suffolk: bogs and marshy lakes.

Given that the online description is, unlike its predecessors, juxtaposed with advertisements for Norfolk Broads holidays, the wording is not only questionable but commercially less than helpful.

Generally the definitions agree on how the Broads got their name, but none of them touch on how they came into being. Forby and Davies would not have known; to them and their peers the Broads were a natural development. It was not until 1952 that any serious doubts were raised. It was then that Dr Joyce Lambert recognised that the steep sides and flat beds of the Broads were the results of ancient peat digging and that they were therefore man-made.

Given how they were made, as well as how they got their name, it's more possible to answer the question, 'What are the Norfolk Broads?'

The Norfolk Broads are a man-made environment, largely the result of ancient peat digging. From their beginnings as a source of fuel they have, over 2,000 years, developed into an area of outstanding beauty and an internationally famous destination for boating enthusiasts, holidaymakers and nature lovers. An essential part of the East Anglian economy, the Norfolk Broads are the largest stretch of wetlands in England.

As a definition that's a good starting point. There is so much more to discover. Let's begin with some facts.

Some Facts

The Broads cover some 117 square miles, mainly in Norfolk, and have over 120 miles of navigable waterways.

Most of them are less than 4 metres (13 feet) deep.

Thirteen of the Broads are open to navigation. Another three have a navigable channel.

There are seven navigable rivers that flow into and out of the Broads: the Bure, the Thurne, the Ant, the Yare, the Chet, the Waveney and the Wensum.

The Broads are wonderfully varied. Despite their name, with its implications of a widened area, they differ enormously in size and shape. Some are small; others, like Hickling Broad and Barton Broad, cover large areas. Consistent with the nineteenth-century descriptions, some of the Broads are integral parts of the river that flows into them, although more typically they can be found to the side of the river, connected to it by a man-made dyke.

The three rivers Ant, Thurne and Bure are in the northern half of the area, and it's here that there are more Broads than in the southern sweep which takes in the rivers Chet, Waveney, Wensum and Yare.

1

Early History and the Romans

Where holidaymakers and local residents now enjoy an area of great natural beauty, picturesque villages, thriving towns and bustling Broads there was once a cruel and unforgiving landscape. Much of the area had been submerged beneath the sea, and as the waters receded, a flat, windswept swathe of land emerged.

Man had come to Norfolk early. There is evidence in the form of flints, bones and tools to show that life was present over 550,000 years ago. Later, weathering the end of the Ice Age, Palaeolithic beings made a life for themselves in the marshy soil.

In the Neolithic period, leading up to 3000 BCE, these distant ancestors had discovered metal. Copper was being worked into tools and utensils during a sociological shift that developed into the Bronze Age. Norfolk was rapidly established as a centre for metalworking. A shield, of copper alloy, was found near Stalham in 1875. It had survived the centuries buried in the very peat that would be excavated to create the Norfolk Broads.

This evolving landscape, where farming was also becoming established, was to be the home of the Iceni.

Occupying roughly the territory we now know as Norfolk, the Iceni were not unsophisticated. They had minted coinage, a social structure and, near present-day Norwich, an established capital city at Venta Icenorum, known today as Caistor St Edmund.

The Romans Are Coming

These early citizens of Norfolk were soon to be part of world history. In AD 43, the Romans made their first visit. It cannot in reality be called an invasion at this stage, as the eminent Roman scholar Tacitus tells us that the Iceni formed an alliance with the Romans, who had arrived under the leadership of Claudius.

The peace did not last. Just four years later, in AD 47, the Roman governor Publius Ostorius Scapula attempted to disarm the Iceni. It created an uprising. The exact site is unknown but a ferocious battle resulted in a Roman victory. The Iceni were, however, allowed to retain their independence.

This meant that their king, Prasutagus, was in effect a Roman puppet or 'client' monarch. As such it was expected that he leave his kingdom to Rome when he died. Pro-Roman as he was, this wealthy man did not toe the line. Instead, seeking to retain his line of descent, he willed his estate jointly to both Rome and his daughters.

The Roman response was swift and harsh. His estates were seized, financial relations were cut, with all loans being called in, and, more terrifyingly, his daughters were raped. They flogged his widow, and in so doing etched the woman's name into history. She was Boudica.

Becoming perhaps the first, and longest-lasting, world-famous name from Norfolk, Boudica sought revenge. With the Roman governor absent while he fought a campaign in Wales, she staged her legendary revolt. She and the Iceni were joined by the Trinovantes, who occupied adjacent territory. This was not a small-scale, nor peaceable, rebellion. Boudica's forces plundered and all but destroyed the Roman towns of Colchester, London and St Albans.

Their strength, fuelled by patriotic indignation, really lay in numbers. The massive force, though initially successful, was ill-disciplined. Outnumbered as they were, the Roman legions were a highly organised, strategically cohesive army. Their victory was inevitable.

It's believed that the defeated Boudica poisoned herself to avoid capture. No concrete evidence of her last days, or even the last battle, exists. As is often the case, the history was written by the victors. Theirs was an emergent civilisation, but the Iceni and ancient Britons of this period had no written literature. It was therefore the Romans who wrote Boudica's story. They were not generous, and they painted a picture of violence and an unwillingness to take prisoners.

In a supreme irony they created a myth: the first English heroine, who would become a cultural touchstone. Falling from notice during the Middle Ages, she would reappear throughout history until the Victorians established her as the logical predecessor and, in poetic terms, 'namesake' of Victoria herself; there is evidence that the name Boudica derives from the Celtic word for victory.

The Romans quickly restored their own regime in Norfolk. The old Iceni capital of Venta Icenorum became a centre of their government. Other settlements appeared, often at the junctions of the Roman-built roads. This was the era of building the sophisticated Roman villas where the wealthy classes lived in considerable comfort.

Away from these 'urban' developments, the rural population began to settle in isolated homesteads, or grouped together in the prototypes of modern villages.

Society was changing. And so was the landscape.

The coastline had been altering for some time but now, slowly at first, the sea level began to fall. What had been swamps dried out, emerging as fertile land. Sheep farming became possible. Salt production was begun. In the westerly reaches of the region, the land settled into the nutrient-rich expanses we know as the Fens.

And in Norfolk the Romans noticed that the land contained large amounts of peat. They knew about peat as a fuel, and they knew how to extract it. A vast supply of it, immediately accessible, was too good to resist. The Romans began to dig it out, leaving the holes that would become the Norfolk Broads.

During the Roman occupation, the peat digging continued unabated. It was an efficient fuel. The area enjoyed relative comfort and prosperity but it was not a time of uninterrupted peace. Raids from Scandinavia and Europe were common. Angles, Saxons and Jutes saw the Romans as wealthy targets, and Norfolk was accessible by sea.

Trade with Europe and the Roman homeland was also by sea, and fortifications were built to protect the shipping that even then went through the towns we now know as Reedham and Great Yarmouth.

Just as the sea levels fell, changing the coastline and creating new land, the Roman Empire seemed to be threatened by erosion itself, worn away by external threats and internal disputes. The legendary discipline was crumbling and disillusion was setting in. So much had changed. By AD 77 the Roman conquest of Britain had been complete. While many Britons had been enslaved, the establishment of Roman customs had brought a degree of civilisation, with roads and houses, laws and flourishing trade. Now, with Rome under attack and the need for all available troops to be there to defend it, the retreat from Britain was inevitable.

By AD 410 there wasn't a Roman soldier left in Britain. Left to defend itself, the country changed. The Roman way of life slowly disappeared. Digging for peat came to a halt.

2

The Middle Ages and Beyond

But, while the Broads were not yet formed, the land around them was taking shape. With the arrival of tribes of Angles, settlements were established. They were split into two factions, the South Folk and the North Folk. Norfolk itself was about to emerge as a recognisable entity.

Norfolk and Suffolk would become part of the kingdom of East Anglia as the various tribes and settlers battled and merged during the post-Roman period. The flat landscape was little more than an expanse of wetlands.

Then, around AD 866, life was in uproar again. The East Anglian coastline witnessed the arrival of a massive Viking force, often referred to as a 'heathen army'. Their leader, Guthrum, conquered, and for a time ruled, the whole of England.

The reality is that the relationship between the local population and the northern invaders was rather more peaceable than legend would suggest. It was also a complex relationship, with history taking some unexpected twists and turns.

It is known, from the contemporary source of the *Anglo-Saxon Chronicle*, that the Vikings, who had been engaged in ferocious fighting as far north as Northumbria, came to Norfolk to settle for the winter. They were not resisted, and evidence suggests that there was indeed some trading between the Angles of Norfolk and the 'invaders'. There are references to horses being traded and a genuine peace being arranged.

It appears to have been short-lived. After little more than three years of coexistence there was an uprising, led by Edmund, effectively the last independent king of East Anglia. The resistance was quelled at a battle near Thetford and Edmund was executed. The location of his vicious killing is disputed, with accounts varying from Suffolk to Hellesdon, just outside Norwich. Wherever he died, his name would reappear following significant developments during the next few years.

It's at this point that a truly legendary name comes in to focus. Alfred, subject of much folklore, had emerged as king and it was he who went into battle against Guthrum, still in place as leader of the Viking people.

Despite his military victory, Alfred was shrewd enough to realise that diplomacy was the way forward. In a strong position for the short term, Alfred realised that he was unlikely to be able to maintain supremacy over the Vikings and he entered into a treaty with Guthrum.

As a direct result of this new state of affairs, the two factions discovered that they had not dissimilar philosophies, and Guthrum converted to Christianity. The executed Edmund now became a saint to those who had killed him.

Lines were drawn, and the nation emerged into a Viking north and a Saxon south. They chose as the divide the old Roman road of Watling Street. Separate identities would be formed and the word 'English' would soon emerge.

In the east, where the Broads were still covered by the marshes and wetland, people were settling. The various migrating social groups, during this long period of development, saw the area as potential farmland, and the earliest seeds of Norfolk's agricultural heritage were sown. Such was the level of settlement that, in contrast to twenty-first-century demographics, the region had become one of the most densely populated areas of the country.

With Vikings, and the English, settling and developing a common interest in agriculture, the country stabilised for a while. Certainly the newcomers found that farming was more hospitable here than in their homeland.

In Norfolk the years around AD 900 saw a growing importance and prosperity. Norwich was emerging as an important centre, perhaps overtaking Thetford, which had hitherto been the flagship settlement in the county.

Such was the continued integration of the two peoples that when, towards the end of the tenth century, another Viking invasion loomed, the resistance to it came from an army comprised of both English and Scandinavian troops.

Skirmishes continued for years and it was only in the reign of Canute, who took over the English crown, that peace finally arrived. The raiders simply stopped coming and the region got on with its business, so much so that, by 1065, times were good. Norwich was a thriving city at the heart of a prosperous and well-populated county.

But 1066 was about to dawn. It was a significant year. It was invasion. Again.

William II of Normandy, enshrined in history as William the Conqueror, had a claim to the English throne through his family ties with the Anglo-Saxon king Edward the Confessor. It's possible that Edward may even have sought to enhance this connection and perceived right. But Edward died in January 1066 and because he had no children the throne passed to Harold II. It was he who defeated the Norwegian army, led by Harald Hardrada, that had landed in northern England in September 1066. The victory was short-lived. Just days later, William landed his army in the south of England. Harold marched south to confront him, and in doing so left much of his force in the North. The armies met at Hastings for the legendary battle that would see Harold killed and the Norman king victorious.

Initially, despite the victory at Hastings, it was not an easy occupation. Rebellions were commonplace and William's strategy to establish control involved seizing land from the old families and giving it to his lords. A direct result of this, and very much part of the plan, was the building of castles to command points of strategic and commercial importance. Norwich Castle stands to this day.

Gradually society began to change. The language and laws altered. The system of government developed. Slavery, which still existed, began to wane.

When the Normans arrived in Norfolk there seems to have been little resistance. The new occupying force soon established itself in the county, the borders of which were already remarkably similar to today's boundaries. The castle was established and would soon be rebuilt and developed. The cathedral was built on the site of what had been the old market; the new market was established on the land that it still occupies, directly beneath the castle.

The religious establishment quickly made its mark. By 1093, the bishop's 'see' was already based in Norwich and records show that in 1121 there was a clear religio-political structure. The Norfolk diocese comprised twelve deaneries including, within Norwich, those of Taverham, Blofield, Ingworth, Sparham, Holt, Walsingham, Toftrees, Brisley, Breckles, Lynn, Thetford and Flegg. Within Norfolk there were Repps, Humbleyard, Depwade, Waxham, Brooke, Redenhall, Rockland, Cranwich, Fencham, Hitcham, Burnham and Hengham. It was a map that remained unchanged until the nineteenth century.

Although life would have been harsh by modern standards, and the rule of law was imposed with severity, Norfolk fared well under Norman rule. Norwich became the central hub of a commercially and politically significant region. For some these were prosperous times. Norfolk was well endowed with churches, many of them still standing, showing the wealth of the ecclesiastical estate. Farms were numerous too and their importance to the economy was vast.

Ever efficient, the Normans began the great survey of their new lands. The Domesday Book gives a fascinating insight into what Norfolk was like at the time. Sheep farming was well established and we know some precise details of it, including a 1,300-strong flock at Walton. Horses were being bred. Salt was being produced in East Flegg and beekeeping was prolific. The leather industry was in place and flourished under Norman rule. Fisheries, clearly seen as valuable, are recorded and the survey lists some 600 watermills.

New civilisation had, however, brought with it the need for shelter and fuel. By the twelfth century much of what is now eastern Norfolk had been plundered of wood in the all-consuming search for building materials and heat. Peat would now emerge again, as it had for the Romans, as a source of fuel.

In an enterprise that would last for 200 years, peat digging was recommenced with commercial zeal. It was big business. The monks of St Benet's Abbey acquired huge rights to peat cutting. It's estimated that the monastery used 200,000 bales of peat a year itself, and there was also a healthy trade in selling the fuel to Norwich and Great Yarmouth.

Though less rugged than some English landscapes, Norfolk can be a cruel environment. In 1287, the county was battered by horrendous storms, causing massive damage. We know that in the December of that year the sea smashed through to inland areas, whipped up by gale-force winds. It flooded farms and fields, roaring through Broadland. Men, women and children were drowned, cattle killed and houses destroyed. Some who survived the initial onslaught took refuge in trees only to succumb to the cold, fall in to the water and die there. At Hickling some 'nine score', or 180, people drowned.

The event was recorded by John of Oxnead. The village would also become the home of the Paston family, whose fifteenth-century letters would detail much of Norfolk life.

Across the next two centuries, millions of cubic feet of peat were dug out of Norfolk. The holes got bigger and bigger. The problem was that the sea levels were getting higher and higher. Water was rushing in to the diggings. As the fourteenth century dawned, the great empty peat pits became flooded, creating numerous expanses of water. It was impossible to continue cutting peat. It would be centuries before this lost and voracious industry was identified as their cause, but the Norfolk landscape now had the Broads.

Meanwhile the dominant industry was certainly agriculture. Norfolk in the fourteenth century was not only the most populous county in England, it was the most intensively farmed. The vast areas that were now available as a result of the medieval clearing of woodland, which in itself had caused the further digging of peat for fuel, were now a prime agricultural resource. Arable farming was good business. With a variety of soil types came a range of crops including rye, oats, peas and barley, which fuelled a burgeoning brewing industry. The emergence of horses as working animals was adopted early in Norfolk and this, coupled with crop-rotation programmes, resulted in an increasingly efficient and productive agriculture. Huge, less productive areas of meadow and pasture, where ploughing and cultivation was less practical, were resourcefully used to support livestock. Sophisticated systems of land management, largely benefiting from the new societal regimes imported by the Normans, meant that crops were transported and marketed by an increasingly affluent class.

The great flat fields of Norfolk were producing food and providing grazing, and in among them it was as if the Broads were sleeping. Their man-made origins were sliding from memory as their original purpose as peat diggings slipped away. They may have been fished, and doubtless their waters were used for agricultural purposes, but this was their quiet time.

It was a quietness not enjoyed by the area as a whole. Despite already being an agricultural area, Norfolk suffered from a dramatic food shortage in the early fourteenth century. As a result, the population was weakened by malnourishment. In such a condition the people had little resistance when, in 1349, the Black Death swept through the county. Somewhere between 30 and 60 per cent of the population of Europe died in the epidemic. In Norfolk, as elsewhere, it wiped out entire villages. Those that remained continued to live by the old methods of 'open-field' farming, with peasants tending their own 'strips' of land. It was a difficult life, made harder by crisis after crisis.

As nature took its relentless course of disease and bad harvests, so others took their opportunity. Wealthier landowners bought or seized land and turned it over for more and more sheep grazing. What had been common land was converted to pasture. It was 'enclosure' and it would lead, as it had with Boudica, to the burning into history of another Norfolk name that stood against domination. Eventually the little men, the peasant farmers, could take no more. They rebelled under the leadership of Robert Kett. It was a brief but glorious struggle. Kett had rallied his forces at Wymondham in July 1549. By December he was dead, hanged at Norwich Castle.

Early in the seventeenth century, Norfolk would live through a grisly rerun of the storm damage of 1287. This time, in 1607, thousands died as once again the sea invaded what we now know as Broadland. Entire villages were washed away, and again vast amounts of livestock were lost. Such was the effect that an Act of Parliament was drawn up in 1609 to enable 'the speedy recovery of many thousand acres of marsh ground … lately surrounded by the rage of the sea'. It had indeed been a raging sea. Damage had been incurred at Horsey, Gillingham, Caister and as far up river as Carrow in Norwich. In Great Yarmouth the Haven Bridge had been destroyed.

Parliament taking action was doubtless rooted in preventing further loss of life in future disasters, but there was a telling commercial note in their paper, which underlines the importance of Norfolk's agricultural significance at the time. The waters, it said, had destroyed 'much hard grounds, and many thousand acres of marsh, upon which great part of the wealth of the county depends'.

This great flood must have been soul destroying for those who survived as, by the early seventeenth century, much of the swampland and many of the rivers had been drained to create the pastures and agricultural land that was the source of so much revenue.

There are glimpses of the wildlife population during this period of change, notably from that eminent, locally based scholar Sir Thomas Browne, who recorded that duck, wigeon and teal were 'plentiful', and that he had seen the bearded titmouse, 'that pretty little fen bird' that would give its name to a little boat much later.

There were otters, too, and 'carrs', which destroyed fish. At Reedham there was a heronry that supplied the king, and near Horsey there were peewits in such numbers that they were taken by the cartload to Norwich, where the citizens used their eggs in puddings. Wildfowling was already established as a profitable business.

Time and again Norfolk was to reel under catastrophe. Within thirty years of Kett's death, a third of the population of Norwich alone would die in the plague of 1579. The Great Plague of 1665 would also take its deadly toll.

With resilience born of necessity, and commerce born from the changes, the county of Norfolk still continued to grow in importance. Sixteenth-century Norwich was second only to London as an English city. Norfolk was producing wool and agricultural products in vast amounts and those goods had to be to be exported from the region. The waterways that would become a favourite holiday destination for future generations were becoming vital conduits of communication and trade.

Norfolk's Broadland in the mid-seventeenth century was a busy place. Cottages and inns were being built, some of them surviving into the twenty-first century. Stalham had its gabled hall by 1670 and many a modern boat is moored at a seventeenth-century inn at Thorpe.

This period of development created an increasing amount of river traffic, and with it came the growing realisation that Norfolk's waterways needed better navigation. Such was the importance of the area that the issue became a topic for government, and on 17 March 1670 an Act of Parliament was passed enabling improvements. It was to have a long-lasting effect, with its main points still in force in the 1930s.

The Act created a new head of navigation at a staithe at Bungay. With locks built at Ellingham, Wainford and Geldeston, the result was a private route, outside the control of the commissioners who had responsibility for most of the rivers.

The inn at Geldeston Lock, still a popular spot, was probably built before this but it certainly saw service as a lock-keeper's cottage before gaining a licence as a public house in the seventeenth century. Beer, especially from Bungay, which had established itself as a brewing town, was transported on the newly improved navigation.

Great Yarmouth also figures in the seventeenth-century history of Broadland for commercial reasons. There is also an interesting insight into how the rivers and Broadland were not exactly devoid of social activity at the time. There had long been an ancient law imposing a levy on the local fishermen for working the lower reaches of the Yare, Bure and Waveney. Always disputed, the legislation was 'challenged' annually at an inquest. The August 1698 inquest was recorded by the diarist and writer the Revd Rowland Davies. He reported a flotilla of wherries, decorated with flags, followed by twenty or more smaller boats. Drums were beaten, men in white caps crewed the wherries, and trumpets were sounded. The formalities involved measuring the mesh of the nets to ensure that fishing was legal, and much archaic language was used during an almost ritualistic performance. It seems, though, that the rest of the population saw this as a water-based festival, with much drinking and celebration.

By now the Broads had their workhorse: the Norfolk wherry. With a history stretching back to 1604, these majestic boats have become an essential part of the story of the Broads.

The Norfolk Wherry

Of all the sights of the Norfolk Broads it's probably the sail of a passing wherry that's most redolent of the area. Wind pumps aside, with a cross of sails standing against the sky, it's the wherry that is inextricably linked to the Broads in the popular imagination.

And yet there are few left, and when they were numerous is beyond living memory. Far beyond living memory are the origins of these craft. The Norfolk keels were big, clinker-built barges. They were powered by a massive square sail and had changed little in design since the Middle Ages. Some say the boats had their origins in craft dating back to the Vikings.

Just as every generation seemingly wants to make things faster, unaware that their predecessors once felt the same, the early nineteenth-century Broads sailors began to let the keel wherry fall from favour. It was a big boat, not easy to manoeuvre, and it needed a big crew. The wherry that began to emerge needed fewer men and it was faster.

The 'trading wherry' that came from these developments had all the features for which a wherry is remembered and known today. It had a tall, single mast, set well forward. It was 'gaff rigged', meaning that the giant sail was four-cornered and controlled by a spar or 'gaff'. The sails were traditionally black.

The 'black-sailed traders' originally had white sails, but they rotted. To prevent this, the crews painted them in herring oil. This proved to be a mistake, as the oil-soaked sails were a delicacy for rats. It was when the sails were finally painted in pitch that the colour, and name, became part of the wherry legend.

Painted black, double-nosed, these boats would work long hours, their white bows picking them out in the dark. They would collect cargo from boats offshore and take it through Broadland. The wherries could handle 25 tons at a time. It seemed that there would always be a place on the Broads for the wherries, but by the time they built the *Ella*, in 1912, the trading days of the wherry were all but over.

The railways were the cause of the trading wherry's end. But, as much as the railways carried goods and freight, injuring the wherry's role, they also brought visitors to the Broads. Resourceful as ever, the Broads folk took practical steps. Wherries were converted to pleasure craft. Initially, with some bedding – often a hammock – and some means of cooking and light, a trading wherry could become a 'pleasure wherry' overnight. It worked. But it was obvious that there was more potential for a worthwhile investment. Soon wherries were being built specifically for pleasure cruising. Some of these craft were constructed to a high standard, with decorative panels on the inside and extensive furniture and equipment. The Colman family, already rich from their legendary mustard, commissioned Hathor, a very luxurious 'pleasure wherry'.

Yet another development was to come. Even the glamorous 'pleasure wherry' was seen as what, in effect, it was: a remodelling of a working boat. Further distancing itself from its origins but steering a straight course to the increasingly demanding holidaymaker came the 'wherry yacht'. These weren't even black. The clean lines of their yacht-style hulls, picked out in white, swept towards a stern on which a safely placed and comfortable seating area allowed holidaymakers to relax without engaging too much in the actual business of hauling sails and suchlike activities.

As lovely as they were, wherries were powered by the wind. A still day meant you stayed still, unless the boat was quanted. A member of the crew would put his shoulder to a long pole, pushing it against the river, or Broad, bed. He'd then walk the length of the craft, forcing it along. As he reached the end, he hauled in the pole and walked back, repeating the process. Quanting was hard work. Perhaps it was hard work watching somebody do it as you lay back in the stern area of a wherry yacht.

But, before they had become pleasure craft the wherries had been the workforce of the Broads. Graceful and fast, they were crewed by men who knew their every trait. At one point over 300 of these giants sailed around Norfolk carrying the cargoes that sustained the county's life. Coal, timber, fish, reeds for thatching and agricultural supplies were all shipped from coast to village, from city to coast.

The great masts were counterbalanced to allow them to be dropped quickly, wasting no time as the bridges were negotiated. Time was of the essence.

Time, however, was stacked against the wherries as commercial carriers. The one that would survive to become the symbol of the Broads' heritage was the *Albion*. Ironically, she was the only one not to be 'clinker built', with overlapping planks in a style that goes back to the Vikings.

3

The Eighteenth Century

The population of the UK in the mid-eighteenth century numbered around 5.7 million. This was not unprecedented, as there had probably been as many people in the country by the mid-fourteenth century. Numbers would rise to similar levels by 1651. The great ebb and flow of population up until this time had been inextricably linked with the availability of food.

Norfolk's part in this economy was noted by Daniel Defoe when he travelled through the county in 1722. He wrote that the River Yare

> passes through the largest and richest tract of meadows in England, stretching from Norwich to Yarmouth, and extended by the marshes on the banks of the rivers Waveney and 'Thym'. On that vast tract of meadows were fed an immense number of black cattle, which not only supplied Norwich, Yarmouth, and the country adjacent with beef, but also great quantities to the London markets.

By 1750 the population was growing faster than ever before and this time food production rose to the challenge of meeting demand. Norfolk was at the heart of the Agricultural Revolution. It was the Norfolk 'Four Course' or rotation system that changed the very nature of arable farming, and, as food production increased, the rivers and Broads of Norfolk continued to be important thoroughfares for trade.

In the heart of Broadland there was much other business activity as well. The year 1770 saw John and Henry Gurney establish their bank in Norwich. It would become Barclays. By 1797, a young merchant called Thomas Bignold had also set up business in Norwich. He called his insurance company Norwich Union. It was a name that would dominate the insurance world, eventually becoming Aviva.

In terms of innovation, 1745 brought a small but important development that will forever be associated with that essential Broadland landmark, the windmill. It was Edmund Lee who, in that year, introduced the 'fan tail' or 'fly'. This is the small wheel that sits on the 'cap' or roof of the mill, at right angles to the sails. Catching the wind's direction, the 'fly', connected by a gearing mechanism, swings the 'cap' around, bringing with it the sails. This meant that the mill would always be turning into the wind, immediately it changed direction. Productivity was greatly increased, and a tiny but vital part of Norfolk's Broadland landscape had been altered forever.

Thriving, and at the forefront in so many ways, Norfolk was, however, not growing in population along with the rest of the country. The dynamics of the nation were beginning to change and the Industrial Revolution that would follow its agricultural predecessor would shift the balance forever.

But the Broads were still busy, and again legislation was brought in to address the problems of navigation. Significant among the various Acts is the one passed in April 1773. This concerned itself with the River Bure and resulted in five new locks being established. Their purpose was to bypass mills at Aylsham, Burgh, Oxnead, Oxnead Lamas and Coltishall.

The full navigation did not materialise until 1779. The entire project was persistently dogged by financial problems. Contractors exceeded their original estimates, which caused delays, further complicated at the other end of the chain by subscribers who defaulted on their promised contributions.

When completed, the works included the planned cut through to Aylsham. There had been a mill at Aylsham since the days of the Domesday Book but it was certainly modified and improved in 1771 by a builder called Robert Parmeter. It's not known if his endeavour was coincidentally, and fortunately, timed or if he was aware of the forthcoming 1773 Act and the building of the 'Aylsham Navigation'.

Although slow to be built, these works were destined for a long life. The wherries plied their trade to Aylsham into the nineteenth century, notwithstanding the arrival of the railways. It was the floods of 1912 that broke the tradition. The locks were badly damaged and, without sufficient funds to repair them, the commissioners closed the section of waterway above Coltishall.

Mid-eighteenth-century Norfolk was a place of change. Not only were the waterways increasingly busy as agriculture became a vital part of the economy of both the county and the country, but the very nature of farming itself was changing. There were virtually none of the old 'strip' fields left. Enclosure had radically changed the landscape. Almost 60 per cent of the county was still used for agriculture, but now the demographic had changed. In the countryside around the Broads there were now wealthy landowners who could afford to indulge in occupations such as specialist stock breeding, which was often a mere diversion as they did not need the revenue from agriculture itself. Tenant farmers were more industrious, but the very intensity of their work meant that smallholders were unable to compete. This was a commercial and competitive race to agricultural riches and the little man was being left behind.

When it was big business, however, it was really big. Geographically well placed to export grain to the Continent, Norfolk shipped tons of it to Holland in particular. Birthplace of agricultural innovations such as crop rotation, Norfolk was a boom place for some, and a grinding uncertainty for others, who now scratched a living much further down the food chain.

Towards the end of the eighteenth century, however, there was a growing feeling of security as far as the elements were concerned.

Despite the sea breaking through, often at Horsey, things settled. There was another storm, which again swept saltwater as far as Norwich, but after the early 1790s the sea was held back for over 100 years.

By this time there was already a list of names that had made Norfolk famous. Boudica and Kett had each fought in bloody conflict on and for the county's soil. Bignold and Gurney had made their long-lasting marks in commerce. Coke and Townsend are names forever linked to agricultural progress.

Now came another. Wars with France had strained the British economy. Inflation was rife. Adding further pressure was the recurrent threat of French invasion, which in turn led to military recruitment drives and an awareness of senior military and naval figures. As much as the nation needed food, and Norfolk was a main provider, it also needed a hero. Norfolk provided that too.

In 1758, a child was born at the rectory in Burnham Thorpe, Norfolk. He would learn to sail on the Broad nearby and go on to become perhaps the most famous sailor, and the most famous Norfolk man, of them all. He was Horatio Nelson.

Horatio Nelson, 1st Viscount Nelson, KB

It is an extraordinary fact that this man, who for many is the epitome of a sailor, learned to harness the wind in a sail on a Norfolk Broad.

He was born in Norfolk, at Burnham Thorpe, in 1758. All his life he would say that he was 'proud to be a Norfolk man'. One of eleven children, Horatio was the son of the Revd Edmund Nelson and his wife, Catherine.

Horatio Nelson's life is well documented. Educated initially at the Paston School in North Walsham, he subsequently attended the King Edward VI Grammar School in Norwich. He was little more than a child when, at thirteen, he joined his uncle's ship, the HMS

Raisonable. His rise to midshipman was almost instant and he was soon being groomed as an officer.

Cursed with chronic seasickness, which stayed with him throughout his life, he progressed well, although his career was not without setbacks. For five years he lived back at his birthplace, Burnham Thorpe, apparently not wanted by the Navy, who had no real work for him in peacetime. Married by then, he led a quiet life in Norfolk, often trying to find work for old shipmates and crew members. However, he was always trying to obtain another command for himself. This and family affairs occupied him until, in 1792, the French Revolutionary government heightened tension by annexing territory belonging to Austria, which had always been seen as a buffer state. Nelson was recalled and given command of HMS Agamemnon. France declared war a month later, in February 1793.

For ten years this brave and talented sailor fought in numerous battles, from Copenhagen to the Nile. He was rewarded for his victories by being created Baron Nelson of the Nile and of Hilborough in the County of Norfolk, which he added to earlier titles, including his being Viscount Nelson of the Nile and of Burnham Thorpe in Norfolk. His connections to his place of birth remained ever strong.

Displaying seamanship and courage that on occasion bordered on the reckless, he was already a hero when he found himself preparing for what has become possibly the most famous sea battle of all time: Trafalgar.

Outnumbered by the combined French and Spanish fleet, but using tactics he'd prepared in the days leading up to the battle, Nelson defeated the enemy but died on the deck of his flagship, HMS *Victory*.

His personal life had not been straightforward, and his affair with Emma Hamilton is as famous as his naval achievements. His place in history, however, is assured because of his skill and courage as a sailor. Possibly the world's most famous sailor, and he learned to sail on a Norfolk Broad.

4

The Nineteenth Century

The first few years of the nineteenth century set the pace for rapid and important change. Politically, the French were no longer threatening to invade England, having been defeated by Nelson in 1805. The United States was becoming larger, having acquired Louisiana. The map of Britain was changing too, with the 1801 Act of Union creating the United Kingdom.

On the domestic and commercial stage, electricity, steam power and railways all made their tentative first appearances as the century geared up for its rush towards a new society.

While in Norwich the new industries were beginning to make their mark, and there was an upsurge in building, there was little discernible change in the Broadland landscape.

The various improvements brought about by late eighteenth-century legislation had proved useful, but agriculturally Norfolk had known better times. Politically it had certainly known easier times.

These were the days of the Corn Law debates and the reform of Game Laws, for which Norfolk magistrates were petitioning loudly. There was also the question of the 1827 Malt Act. Prominent local politician and agriculturalist 'Farmer' Coke had spoken for Norfolk's farmers, who were furious at the regulations the Act imposed on them, including the stopping of their traditional technique of wetting barley to be used as cattle fodder.

It was an era of volatile politics. The renowned Edmund Wodehouse, MP for Norfolk, was physically attacked in 1826. He was on his way to entertain his supporters when he was set upon by the 'anti-Catholic' mob. Their anger was fuelled by Wodehouse having spoken out against measures that levied extra taxation on Catholics. He had also just spoken regarding the proposed 'Norwich and Lowestoft Navigation'. On to the stage comes the engineer William Cubitt.

Cubitt was a Norfolk man. Born in 1785, he had begun his working life apprenticed to a cabinetmaker in the heart of the Norfolk Broads, at Stalham. His career would include becoming chief engineer at Ransomes in Ipswich, building the South Eastern Railway and acting as consulting engineer for the Great Northern Railway. In 1851, as president of the Institution of Civil Engineers, he would oversee the building of the Great Exhibition building in Hyde Park, and gain a knighthood for it.

In a career that saw him invent a type of windmill sail and threshing equipment, as well as being involved with some of the massive Victorian construction projects, Cubitt also left a darker legacy: he invented the treadmill. Initially he had seen it as a means of using prison labour to grind corn. Having employed prisoners, he believed that their labour could be put to good use. He did not foresee the use of the treadmill as a means of punishment.

It was his usually rather more reliable foresight that was often called on following his experience with railway building. His expertise was also sought by parliament in relation to the proposed work in Norfolk, the county of his birth.

He was not alone. Other leading figures in civil engineering were also called, among them Thomas Telford and Alexander Nimmo. The strategic vision for the project was to provide a better, more direct, route between Lowestoft and Norwich. Up until the 1820s cargo had been carried by vessels that sailed the Yare, out through Breydon Water, before picking up the River Bure near Great Yarmouth. The nature of Breydon Water, with its wide area of shallow water, required special craft. That meant transferring cargo in Great Yarmouth before onward shipping to Norwich.

In Norwich the merchants were unhappy at this situation. The costs of this 'trans-shipment' were an added burden, but also there were suspicions of pilferage. When eighteen men were convicted of theft, William Cubitt was called in. It wasn't the first time. He had originally been asked to look at the problem in 1814, when he'd suggested dredging a deep channel at the southernmost edge of Breydon Water.

At that time his estimated costs were £35,000, and when his plan was published in 1818 Great Yarmouth Corporation instantly objected and sought a second opinion. They called on a respected engineer called John Rennie, who suggested that the plan had a flaw that would result in the silting up of Great Yarmouth's harbour. The challenge was passed back to Cubitt, who came up with a scheme to link the Yare to Lowestoft, this time at an estimated cost of £70,000.

There were more objections, but a Bill was put before parliament in 1826. It was defeated. The second Bill, of May 1827, was passed. Protests continued, and there were campaigns against it in Great Yarmouth, but the Act, which created the Norwich and Lowestoft Navigation Company, was passed by parliament in May 1827.

The concept was for a 2-mile cut, or canal, that would link the rivers Waveney and Yare, by running from Reedham to Haddiscoe. Cubitt proposed locks at Munford Bridge, built to include gates that faced both ways. He also advocated the use of steam powered tugs. Dredging work began straight away, and although there were problems, the 'cut' was opened in 1833.

Despite the long political fight, the dredging of parts of the River Yare and the construction of Oulton Dyke, the project was not a commercial success. By 1842, the Haddiscoe Cut had been taken over by the Exchequer Loan Commissioners. They sold it to the railway developer Sir Morton Peto.

Sir Morton Peto

Peto is a giant of the Victorian age. His achievements include building the Reform Club and the Lyceum in London, the construction of the Grand Crimean Central Railway, in 1854, to support troops in the front line and building the Grand Trunk Railway in Canada. Born in 1809, he had seen the potential in railways as early as 1834, when he set himself up, in partnership with his cousin, as an independent railway contractor. They won significant projects including stations in Birmingham and sections of the Great Western Railway.

His connections with Norfolk and the Broads are an interesting sequence of coincidences. Firstly, prior to his railway work, he had built one of London's most famous landmarks. Peto had built Nelson's Column, a monument to national hero Horatio Nelson, who had learned to sail on the Norfolk Broads.

Secondly, Peto was much involved with the Great Exhibition of 1851. Acting as guarantor for some of the financing, he was, even if indirectly, enabling the work of William Cubitt, whose evidence had influenced the building of the Haddiscoe Cut, which Peto himself would subsequently buy.

Peto's name would also become linked with another notable Norfolk name. The novelist George Borrow became locked in a dispute with him over a railway line that the great engineer wanted to run through part of Borrow's land at Oulton Broad.

Morton Peto moved to East Anglia in 1844, buying Somerleyton Hall, in Suffolk. Knighted for his services during the Crimean War, he became Baronet of Somerleyton Hall and served as Liberal MP for Norwich from 1847 to 1854. At one point Peto was the largest employer of labour in the world. And yet by 1868 he was bankrupt and forced to give up his seat in parliament. He tried to work abroad, and later in Cornwall, but he failed. He died in obscurity in 1889. His name lives on in Broadland, as Peto's Marsh can still be found on the map, near Oulton Dyke.

Peto's move to the area in 1844 is coincident with the great upsurge in railway-building activity at this time. The Broads were already beginning to develop as a place for recreation, and regattas and races had been taking place since the late eighteenth century. By the 1830s, the various races and 'water frolics' were more widespread and better-attended. Still largely the preserve of the upper and middle classes, these recreational activities began to take on a competitive edge. Racing was taken seriously and inevitably spawned designs for faster craft.

Notable among these was the lateener. Quite how this graceful design, named after its triangular rig, came to be such a feature of the Norfolk Broads is not really known. The lateen rig had been used as far afield as the Barbary Coast, the Nile and on Venetian galleys. It had, because of its manoeuvrability, been used on English galleons until the gaff rig replaced it.

On the Broads, the lateener appears to have arrived with a craft built by Etheridge's at Norwich in 1818. It was fast and had real sailing advantages. The design was taken up by other boatbuilders, and similar craft were soon to be seen around the Broads.

It is perhaps in the first half of the nineteenth century that the Broads began to reveal the social diversity that would be part of their development. An important figure in this area was John Harvey. If the lateener had had some distant connection with Venice, Harvey would bring a more direct influence from that culture. He was a successful Norwich merchant and he had been to Venice as part of the Grand Tour. This traditional trip around Europe, taken by the comfortably off to further their cultural education, would, like the Broads, change by the 1840s, when railways revolutionised travel.

Harvey had seen the waterside festivities in Venice and brought the idea to Norfolk. Begun in 1824, the Thorpe Water Frolics became a huge attraction. Crowds of over 30,000 people would gather, the day becoming an annual treat for the weavers and workers of the city. Harvey's fortune was largely based on textiles and he had also been heavily involved in the movement to make Norwich a significant port. Full of commercial zeal, he was also patron of the arts.

Running through the evolution of the Broads, like the constant flow of the rivers, is a sense of contrast and balance. There is the constant weighing of the commerce and the conservation. The retention of the natural beauty of these wetlands is always set against their development as places of recreation. The desire to keep them for the pleasure of the local inhabitants is kept in perspective by the need to attract visitors and the business they represent. There is the social issue of the Broads being a playground for the better-off, as opposed to their accessibility to all; an issue of demographics that recurs throughout the great changes in society in the nineteenth and twentieth centuries.

The Thorpe Water Frolics give us perhaps the first real insight in to this complex picture, and they do it, quite literally, with a picture. Harvey was so pleased with the Frolics that he commissioned a painting of them. The artist he chose to capture the scene was Joseph Stannard.

The Norwich School of Painters

The origins of the Norwich School can be traced back to 1803. Arguably the first provincial art movement in Britain, the Norwich School is also worthy of note for its members being working class, largely self-taught and without significant patronage.

Founded by John Crome and Robert Ladbrooke, the group took some influences from the great Dutch landscape painters. Their real inspirations, however, were the encouragement of one another and the landscapes of Norfolk.

Given that their first meeting was held in the 'Hole in the Wall' tavern, their avowed aims were quite lofty. Their purpose was, they said, to hold 'an enquiry into the rise, progress and present state of painting, architecture, and sculpture, with a view to point out the best methods of study to attain the greater perfection in these arts'. Within two years the group had grown and moved premises. It now afforded members a place to work and show their pictures. The first exhibition was held in 1805, and it became an annual event for the next twenty years. The 1825 exhibition was the last for three years, as the building the school occupied was demolished.

This was the year that Stannard's Thorpe Water Frolic was first shown. As a young man, Stannard had approached Crome in the hope of gaining tuition. Crome's refusal, which led to Stannard breaking away from the group, was to haunt him. His family and friends never forgave him for snubbing Stannard.

It's interesting to note that in his *Thorpe Water Frolic, Afternoon* of 1825, Stannard includes a detail of a little boy pulling a toy boat, from the stern of a real craft. It's the very same cameo that appears in Crome's painting Back of New Mills, Evening which he'd painted possibly as early as 1812.

Crome, who had most certainly been the central figure of the Norwich School, died in 1821. Although the group now included names such as Stannard, Stark and Crome's son 'Young Crome', it was John Sell Cotman who emerged as the new leader.

The quality of their work is beyond question. These vigorous, attractive paintings of Norfolk are important works of art. Perhaps glimpsing briefly backwards to some European influence, they equally – certainly in the case of Cotman's watercolours – anticipate the broad washes of Impressionism.

Although the work of the Norwich School of Painters is now world-famous, it was not always so. In a twist of fate, it's possibly because of some local support, rather than the lack of it, that the paintings did not immediately make their creators as famous as other names from the era, such as Constable and Turner. J. J. Colman, industrialist, philanthropist and namesake for his world-famous mustard, collected most of the Norwich School canvasses. Retained in Norwich, they suffered from a lack of national exposure until a major Tate Gallery exhibition in London in 2001.

The Norwich School continued under Cotman's leadership until he left Norwich in 1834. He went to take up post at King's College School, and with his departure the Norwich School ceased to be an entity.

Stannard was part of the Norwich School. Born in Norwich, he had achieved critical success but was suffering financially. Perhaps this, coupled with his being a keen and skilled oarsman, prompted Harvey to choose him. The painting, *Thorpe Water Frolic, Afternoon*, was first shown in 1825.

It shows firstly the sheer size of the crowd. The tens of thousands there almost certainly outnumber the population of Norwich at the time, suggesting that people travelled to be at Thorpe. It's also such a big crowd that it must have drawn men, women and children from a range of backgrounds. The social division is further marked by the gentry occupying the left bank while the workers watch from the right. Stannard, despite his financial position, owned a boat, the *Cytherea*. It's shown in his picture, crewed by working lads, some of them in uniform.

For all its eclectic make-up and bustling activity, the afternoon at Thorpe Water Frolics captured in Stannard's masterpiece is still a scene from the 1820s. Although in Norwich there was an industrial base, the weavers were facing recession, and were still working from their homes. In the rural areas, and in Broadland, life had remained much the same. The Industrial Revolution had not made the impact it had elsewhere, largely owing to the geographical fact of Norfolk's isolation.

All of that would change from 1844. The railways arrived.

The Coming of the Railways

It was seen as a watershed from the outset. Even in August 1844, the *Norfolk Chronicle* reported that 'about 60 cwt of tea and coffee' had been brought to Norwich by the Yarmouth & Norwich Railway Company, for Messrs Wolton and Co., of London Street. 'We should not be surprised,' said the newspaper, 'that if that practice become more general in busy weeks, particularly when the wind is contrary for the favourable transit of the wherries.'

The winds of change were indeed blowing. But, the arrival of railways had been met with nothing but optimism. Earlier that year, on 30 April, the *Norfolk Chronicle* had reported that

> the Yarmouth and Norwich Railway was formally opened on this date. The county was indebted to Mr. R. Stephenson, the celebrated engineer and 'father of railways', for the introduction of the line.

This was indeed the case. Sir Morton Peto, now operating from offices in Norwich, was the contractor. In fact George Stephenson, the even more famous father of Robert, who was chief engineer, was the original chairman of the company when it was formed, by Act of Parliament, in 1842.

The first meeting of proprietors had been held at the Victoria Hotel, in Great Yarmouth, on 5 August 1842, where the cost of the line's building had been estimated at £200,000. Peto, with his partner Grissell, were to be the constructors at a cost of £10,000 per mile.

The *Norfolk Chronicle* painted a lively picture of the first day's business:

> Thousands of persons assembled at Thorpe Station to witness the departure of the first train at 10.30, hundreds thronged the line at various points, and a great crowd gathered at Yarmouth to see the arrival. Howlett's brass band occupied a third-class carriage next the engine, and the other carriages were reserved for 200 guests, specially invited by the directors. The train started amid loud cheers, and accomplished the journey in 50½ minutes; the return trip was done in 44 minutes.
>
> At four o'clock a dinner was held at the Assembly Rooms, Norwich, under the presidency of Mr. S. M. Peto, supported right and left by the Mayors of Norwich and Yarmouth. The railway was opened for public traffic on May 1st, when 1,015 passengers were booked.

The railways had definitely arrived in Norfolk. As they did everywhere else, they spread. By the 1870s, the East Norfolk

Railway Company was in operation. Opening in 1874, the company was focused on the north Norfolk town of Cromer. This was becoming a popular resort with Victorian holidaymakers, and with rail connections from London to Norwich the potential was enormous.

Trains would run out of Norwich, following the lines of the Yarmouth & Norwich railway. It's here, east of Norwich that the railways will reappear in the literature of the Broads. It's also here, in 1874, that one of the worst railway disasters in British history occurred. Brought on from Brundall, in a calamitous break in communications, a train crashed head-on in to the train coming out of Norwich.

The East Norfolk Railway trains left the Yarmouth & Norwich line at Whitlingham Junction to head north for Cromer. Just over 8 miles from Norwich they stopped at a small village called Wroxham. It was to be all change for the Broads.

Wroxham: Capital of the Broads

In a geographical fact that typifies how Norfolk is full of idiosyncrasies, of which Norfolk people are proud, Wroxham station is not in Wroxham. It is in fact situated in the adjacent village of Hoveton and is, officially, Hoveton and Wroxham station. There have been some who have pointed out that the title 'Capital of the Broads', often attributed to Wroxham, is unjust. It's Hoveton where the business is done. The name of Wroxham, though, is firmly marked on the map of the Norfolk Broads.

Wroxham has a long history. Its bridge, famous for being one of the most difficult to navigate on the Broads, dates back to ancient history. There was certainly a wooden bridge by 1576 and the current brick-and-stone structure replaced that in 1619.

The Grade I listed church of St Mary the Virgin was dramatically restored by the Victorians but is of Norman origin, with a twelfth-century doorway.

The village is located in a loop of the River Bure, between Belaugh Broad to its west and Wroxham Broad to the east. Hoveton, the adjacent village, is on the northern side of the Bure.

In the nineteenth century, when the railway reached Wroxham, it was a quiet, rural place. North of the city of Norwich and south of the coast it was a village surrounded by agricultural land. However, activities on the river and Broad had already commenced.

There is an account, for instance, from 1865, by Walter White, who says of a regatta there that 'the Broad is all animation ... The broad grassy staithe is thronged by people who have come on foot or on wheels, thickest about the booth where cakes and ale are to be had.'

His description goes on to embrace the same diverse spread of people, and their attitudes to the Broads, which had been captured earlier by Stannard and would go on to characterise the area for decades to come.

> And soon after this [the starting gun] three cutters start to sail round the course ... Some of the yachts display flags enough for a whole fleet, and their decks are thronged with spectators, among whom appear the comely faces of English maidens, and the wherries, with their double rows of seats closely packed, exhibit company of all degrees ... except a few yachtsmen and wherrymen there seems to be no one who takes an interest in the sailing match ... if constant eating and drinking may be taken as evidence, dinner time lasts all day.

Gradually this level of activity was to increase. Although a wide cross section of people were engaging in recreation on the Broads, they were still predominantly local folk. Now, as the railways brought more people in to the area, a different picture began to emerge.

Great Yarmouth and the rather more fashionable Cromer were still important destinations. Rail travel made them even more accessible, and the relative calm of Norfolk held a significant appeal to people from the increasingly busy towns and cities. The seaside holiday was becoming a part of British life for more and more people. Once available only to the better-off, they were now affordable for, and offered welcome relief to, the working class.

Travelling through Norfolk to reach its north coast, and often stopping off, or simply observing the Broads from the train, the more affluent classes began to realise that the Broads represented a new kind of holiday. Here was something mildly adventurous, yet not overly taxing. This was somewhere that one could relax in some style and be away not just from work but also from the 'other people' who had started to share the seaside resorts.

These middle-class Victorians had begun a love affair with eating out of doors and relaxing in the 'natural environment'. Wroxham was a very convenient place of entry. As the trade and the potential grew, among others, two astute businessmen watched.

The Beginnings of Boat Hire

John Loynes had served an apprenticeship in Bungay before moving to London. Provincial life suited him better and he moved to Norwich where he opened for business as a master carpenter. A keen amateur sailor, he spent a lot of time on the River Wensum, and used his skills to build his own boat. He took the boat to Wroxham. Legend has it that he dragged it there in a handcart. Having experienced different waters, he constructed a bigger boat. This proved attractive to his friends, some of whom asked if he would 'rent' it to them for a holiday. Sometime around 1878 he let them do just that and at that moment, arguably, created the Norfolk Broads boat-hire business.

Loynes didn't stop there. At his Norwich premises he built more boats and hired them out as well. However, he noticed that, just like himself, many customers preferred to tackle the more northern waters. This meant that they often left the boats for him to collect from Wroxham.

This was a clear sign. By 1888, Loynes had moved his business to Wroxham. Ever resourceful and astute, he began to meet market requirement and tastes by building a new kind of boat. These were cabin yachts, with a roof that could be raised and lowered. It was a late nineteenth-century innovation but it's still evident in boat design today.

Loynes' cabin yachts also had sleeping and cooking facilities on board. That meant that there was a need for 'supplies'. This was a fact that did not go unnoticed by another local business.

Roys of Wroxham

Alfred and Arnold Roy were brothers who had started business with a general store in Coltishall in 1895. Backed by their father, on the condition that they worked together in the venture, the Roys became the village shopkeeper and postmaster respectively. Prospering from Coltishall's buoyant economy, which was driven by the malting industry, they sought to expand. They took a second shop in Dereham, and then a third in Hoveton, just across the river from Wroxham.

They too noticed that there was a new trade. The same relatively affluent, middle-class holidaymakers that John Loynes had seen were not just passing through, but using the train to get to Wroxham, where they hired boats. Initially these were often skippered wherries, but Loynes, and George Smith at the Horse Shoes Hotel on the river, were now hiring out smaller craft.

This had to be an enormous opportunity. Starting from the basic idea of having in stock what the holidaymakers wanted before they 'set sail', the Roys soon developed the concept into the bigger idea of fully provisioning their boats before the visitors arrived at the railway station. It worked. The business grew, and as it did so supplies to the shop would also reach Wroxham by rail.

By then the railway companies had been 'grouped' into larger organisations. The eastern part of the UK was serviced by the

London & North Eastern Railway. Despite the Hoveton location, consignments by rail would be addressed to 'Roy Brothers, LNER Station, Wroxham'. Similarly, telegrams would be dispatched to 'Roy Brothers Wroxham'. It was a short step to the now famously alliterative 'Roys of Wroxham', a business that has flourished to become an integral part of the Broads, and a contributory factor in Wroxham itself gaining the title 'Capital of the Broads'.

As the Victorians began to enjoy the Broads, seeing it as a rural and sequestered idyll, they were, of course, ironically, travelling there by train, that very symbol of the industrial age from which they sought to escape. Not all technological advances of the nineteenth century were concerned with steaming locomotives, thundering looms and flying shuttles, though; there were quieter innovations and discoveries that have had equally dramatic long-term effects.

Words and Pictures

As early as 1790, Thomas Wedgwood had experimented with photography. The world's first known photograph had been created by 1826, when Nicéphore Niépce captured his *View from the Window at Le Gras*. As refinements made it possible for photographers to carry their equipment with them, it was inevitable that the 'great outdoors' would provide subject matter for them.

The open spaces of the Broads began to appear in photographs during the late nineteenth century. Often called 'the man who found the Broads', G. Christopher Davies (1849–1922) was among the first to capture Broadland scenes with a camera. He was a writer too, and his *The Handbook to the Rivers and Broads of Norfolk and Suffolk* is a vital part of Broads history.

Published in 1882, it ran to some fifty editions. With great, and seemingly typical, foresight, one man advertised his business in the first edition. He recognised the potential and future in publicising the Broads. It was John Loynes.

Davies published other works, including *The Swan and Her Crew*. This children's novel is set at Hickling and is undoubtedly an influence on later Broads-based literature. The overall quality of Davies' photography is a matter of some debate. Invaluable as they are as a pictorial record, they perhaps lack the professionalism that would soon be a measure for the medium.

His writing, however, can sometimes capture an image of the Broads with stunning accuracy and create a timeless picture in itself. Long before the millions of postcards and posters that would portray this scene, Davies said of a wherry sailing through Norfolk, 'The course of the river through the green marshes is, where the water is itself invisible, marked by the tall high-peaked sails of these craft, which seem to be gliding along the land itself.'

Davies is without question a significant figure in the development of the Broads. He is not, however, the originator of Broads writing and literature. Who wrote the first words, or created the first picture, will never be known for certain. In terms of a 'modern' writer who would serve to popularise the Broads, great credit must be given to Davies' predecessor Walter White. His *Eastern England from the Thames to the Humber* appeared in 1865. The chapters on the Broads are well written and sensitively observed.

His work is in the style of a 'travel log', and this method would be developed by other writers, including C. A. Campling, whose 1871 book *The Log of the Stranger* was another catalyst for a stream of similar, and now dated, stories of boating. In 1882, the year that Davies published his handbook, almost creating the concept for such guides, a young man called Peter Henry Emerson began experimenting with photography.

Emerson was born in Cuba and had moved to England in 1869 when his father died. The family was wealthy, having owned a sugar plantation, and Peter was sent to King's College London and then Clare College, Cambridge, from where he graduated with a medical degree in 1885.

At some point in 1882 he had acquired a camera which, originally, he intended to use on his birdwatching forays. However, photography itself became the primary interest. An early adopter of the notion of photography as art, he gave up his medical career to concentrate on it. His influence was very much the French artists who sought to capture natural scenes, and Emerson believed that the pursuit of sharply focused photographs of rural and natural life would form a vital and realistic record.

For his first album of photographs he produced forty platinum prints of *Life and Landscape on the Norfolk Broads*. The pictures achieve his objective in showing life as it would be seen by the naked eye. Here was a still relatively new technology being used to capture images of an old life and disappearing world.

The world that was emerging was one of more leisure time, commercial activity and the beginnings of tourism as we know it today. G. C. Davies' works had certainly helped to 'market' the Broads and his often used title of 'the man who found' or sometimes 'discovered' the Broads did not always sit easily. There is a sense almost of guilt that he had opened up the area to a greater public and in doing so had, in a way, helped change the very thing he loved.

Later editions of his *Handbook*, and other books, would include pieces on angling and types of boat, birds and wildlife to increase people's knowledge of the Broads. However, simultaneously he would bring in some warning notes that again strike the balance between commercial recreation and sensitive conservation. There were his rules of etiquette for the Broads, which included the discouragement of 'songs and revelry after eleven p.m. and bathing after eight a.m.'. There are suggestions as to conduct concerning 'ladies' and a reminder that 'sound travels a long way on the water'.

One should not, he says, 'criticise people you may encounter with too loud a voice'. This is oddly ambiguous for so skilled a writer. Does he mean one should not criticise people who have a loud voice? Or does he mean one should not use a loud voice oneself to criticise people of whom one might not approve? Either way, it's an interestingly sensitive comment which again hints at the balance and contradictions of Broads behaviour and, with telling foresight, sets the scene for contrasts that will reappear time and again in the coming decades.

Chronologically it's the next author of the Broads who begins to embrace some of the practical aspects of cruising for a holiday. Ernest Suffling's *The Land of The Broads* first appeared in 1885. It was very much concerned with an audience who 'take an interest in one of the quaintest and most old-world parts of England'. The book was a best-seller, but he did not stay with the formula. His second work, published in 1891, was much more pragmatic.

How to Organise a Cruise on the Broads was unusual. Suffling made it plain that he considered the book to be an improvement on previous guides, and that he was drawing on long and informed experience. This was quite a robust stance given the number of works available, some of them, like Davies', notable.

The step change came with the inclusion of details about food and drink in the area. It was not always positive. He thought that bacon was not always good in Norfolk, and he had firm views on the quality, or lack of it, of Norfolk ale and whisky.

Suffling also went on to give hints and advice on caring for equipment and clothes. Fishing boots apparently could be best dried out by stuffing them with barley grains, which will swell because of the moisture and stop the boots from cracking.

There are suggestions for games and entertainments, including, on larger yachts, hiring a piano for fifteen shillings a day.

Among the relatively predictable guidance on routes and sailing techniques, though, come some pointers for cooking on boats. The holiday was moving toward the 'self-catering' of later days, and the written word was now endorsing what the Roys and Mr Loyne had intuitively seen as the future.

The curious balance of the Broads was still evolving. While Suffling's *How to Organise a Cruise on the Broads* was arriving on the bookshop shelves with its modernising advice, P. H. Emerson was sailing the Broads in his converted wherry *Maid of the Mist*, engaged with taking photographs of the scenery and its inhabitants, determined to capture the 'real' Norfolk.

The sixteen pictures from this trip were published as his last work, entitled *Marsh Leaves*. Exquisite and atmospheric, featuring the Broads in winter as well as summer, the photographs are a truly sensitive record.

Emerson's enthusiasm for his calling was immense and deep. Spilling over from pure observance, he involved himself with the local population to the extent of joining poachers on their treks. Subsequently, he was called a 'socialist' for his public stance of criticising the sentences handed out to poachers. This was a contentious view, as the benches who handed out the convictions were usually comprised of the owners of the land on which the poaching took place.

Emerson's empathy with the workers and his sensitive, natural, pictures were in contrast to both the opinions and good – but frankly, often posed – photographs of Davies. Both men loved the Broads, but the weighing of different viewpoints, and the evolving nature of society, was still at the heart of changing Norfolk.

An example of the worlds of art and commerce coming together is found in the work of the photographer John Payne Jennings. A Surrey man, he was a public servant, working at least part-time for the parish council. Interestingly, G. C. Davies served as clerk to the county council after he returned to Norfolk in 1889.

Jennings was commissioned by the fledgling advertising department of the Great Eastern Railway Company to take pictures of the Norfolk Broads. The format he used was designed to fit the frames above the seats in the railway carriages, where they saw considerable exposure. The photographs were subsequently published as an album, by Jarrolds, in 1885, with a second volume soon after.

Of a certain quality, and evocative of the Broads atmosphere, the pictures were never accompanied by his own words. In the first album there is an advertisement for the Great Eastern Railway, understandably endorsing their investment. In the second volume there are captions, provided by Suffling, somehow cementing the commercial bond between the two, while Emerson stands alone and esoteric.

Though Emerson's photographs are almost mystical, they represent real life. They are factual. By the late nineteenth century, the Broads appear in literary fiction as well. In 1866, the year in which further legislation was enacted for the Broads, Wilkie Collins, friend of Dickens and author of *The Moonstone* and *The Woman in White*, placed some of his novel *Armadale* at 'Hurle Mere'. This is without doubt a fictionalised version of Horsey Mere. It's a sensitive portrayal of what he sees as a mysterious region. It's also an indication of a growing awareness of the Broads, even if they were still characterised as remote.

It was a remoteness at risk. The late nineteenth century was rushing toward fundamental shifts. The railways were having an impact on waterborne freight. With a resourcefulness that would be employed again, as other changes arose, boat owners and builders began to see the need to diversify. Cruising and recreation marked the inevitable new course to steer, and with them came the need for the other pleasures and services that Norfolk's new visiting, and local, public would need.

This growth in tourist or holiday activity could be seen at places such as Somerleyton Hall. Sir Samuel Morton Peto had bought the house and carried out extensive work on it in the 1840s before his bankruptcy. He sold the hall to the wealthy son of the founder of Crossley Carpets. Once, Peto had been the largest employer of labour in the world. Now, his friend Sir Francis Crossley would develop Crossley Carpets to become one of the largest manufacturing organisations of its kind in the world. Like Peto, Crossley would serve as an MP. But now, Crossley was in Peto's old home and in the late nineteenth century, during the summers, he opened the doors of Somerleyton Hall to the public.

At Brundall Gardens, 18 acres of shrubs and trees were planted by Dr Michael Beverley. By the 1920s, as the holiday era developed, an extra railway station would be opened at Brundall Gardens to deal with the numbers of visitors to the gardens and surrounding area, which included the village of Brundall, itself a place deeply rooted in Broads history.

At Bramerton Woods End, there had been an inn since the seventeenth century. In the 1820s Joseph Stannard, who had painted the *Thorpe Water Frolic*, completed his canvas of *Boats on the Yare near Bramerton, Norfolk*. By the end of the nineteenth century, the inn would boast tea gardens and establish itself as a typical and attractive spot for holidaymakers and day trippers from Norwich.

Tearooms and places for hiring rowing boats, woodland walks and sites for picnics all sprang up at inns and riverside pubs.

Fritton Lake was another location to offer refreshments and boats, along with the Eels Foot Inn at Ormesby. By 1897, the Swan at Horning was completed, although there had been an inn there for centuries.

It Pays to Advertise

In the 1890s, another measure of the commercial growth of the Broads as a holiday destination became apparent. The Great Eastern Railway Company had already made serious inroads into marketing themselves by promoting the area. This technique would continue ever after as rail, ship and later airline companies would sell the attractions of a destination because it is more appealing than the act of being taken there. Selling the place first and what to do there second is a proven strategy in advertising. The advertising of the late nineteenth century gives a clear idea of how boating holidays on the Broads were growing.

In the first edition of G. C. Davies' *Handbook* in 1882, the only advertisement it carried was that of the pioneering John Loyne. In the 1890s, the later editions carried over thirty advertisements for 'boats for hire'.

The seventh edition of Suffling's *Land of the Broads* came out in 1895. It contained over fifty advertisements for yachts and wherries for hire. Suffling took his involvement a stage further. In a prototypical move for later developments, he set himself up as an 'agent'. He would take the responsibility of hiring out boats, and crew, to customers, on behalf of yards he trusted. By the end of the 1890s he had a full order book and a growing offering of boats including wherries, yachts and houseboats.

If more evidence that this was a growing industry was needed, it comes from Davies himself. At about this time, he commented that, although there was good accommodation to be had at the local inns and houses, it was 'too meagre' and 'insufficient for demand'. It was hardly surprising. The books, the guides, the newspaper and magazine articles, the photographs and the advertising had all, directly and indirectly, taken awareness of the Broads to an unprecedented level. Conditions and pay, although not universally, had improved. The railway made travel easier and available to a wider public.

As life became noisier and more hectic, the Broads represented, for some, a welcome idyllic contrast. For others, it was a new place for new activities. For fun.

The boatbuilders, the shopkeepers, the publicans, the innkeepers, the railway directors, the publishers and the public were all primed. The twentieth century was just around the corner.

5

The First Half of the Twentieth Century

1900–1910

With evidence of life dating back over half a million years, it's hardly surprising that the Broads did not change overnight at the turn of just another century. The reality is that, as the twentieth century arrived, many aspects of life on the Norfolk Broads didn't change at all. Although its importance was now much diminished, there was still some peat being dug. Certainly it was still being sold in modest quantities at Horning around 1900.

While the boatyards and inns, tearooms and railways began to fall in step with the 1900s, some on the Broads still trod the measured pace of an earlier era – none more so than the marsh men.

There was no single trade for these tough Broadland dwellers. Their origins are lost in time, but well into the early twentieth century, out in the marshes, they continued to make their living from either the reeds or cattle. Linking the two occupations was that of physically maintaining the dykes and mashes. There was a rhythm to this long-established lifestyle.

The cold, demanding work of reed cutting would start just before Christmas. Using scythes, specially modified with a hoop for collecting the reeds, the marsh men would cut and bind the stems. Sometimes they would work from a boat; often from the shore. It was a gruelling task. After it was cut, a bundle of reeds, known as a 'shofe', had to be cleaned and combed. Five of these would then be tied together with a reed. These bigger bundles were enormous. They measured 6 feet in diameter, which is presumably why they were known as 'fathoms'. (A fathom being a maritime measure of 6 feet of depth in water.) Cutting and tying ten, fifteen or more of these in a day was back-breaking. The pace was insistent as the unit of selling was 120 fathoms.

The reeds would be sold primarily for thatching, in itself a skilled occupation. One of the finishing touches to a Norfolk thatched roof was the way in which the ridges would be worked with sedge, another part of the marsh man's harvest.

By early spring the reed harvest was over. March would see a period of renewing and bidding for leases on marshland farmsteads, and by April the marsh men would be buying cattle. The beasts were not always locally reared, as they had been in centuries before, when the same land was common grazing. Now they were often Scots cattle, brought down in droves to be auctioned at a large annual sale held at Horsham St Faith on the northern edge of Norwich.

Through the spring and summer these cattle would be tended and grazed, producing high-quality beef. During these months the marshes needed constant attention, and pumps were watched and worked to ensure that the dykes retained enough water for the cattle, but not so much as to cause flooding.

As winter set in, with the cattle gone, there was more hard work to do in cleaning, dredging and maintaining the dykes and ditches before, as Christmas approached, the cycle came round again to harvesting the reeds.

By any modern standards this was not only a hard life, but also one lived in less-than-congenial conditions. The marsh men and their families lived in small cottages, usually with a single room on the ground floor and perhaps two or more small bedrooms upstairs. Dark and uncomfortable as these thatched cottages were, it was inevitable that they appeared as quaint to the outsider.

And now, there were more outsiders.

Well before the end of the nineteenth century, members of the Norwich School had ventured out to paint in the open air and capture Broadland as a rural idyll of old England.

By 1891, Emerson had visited the marsh men and taken his sympathetic and evocative photographs. Part of their poignancy is that it's obvious these are pictures of a disappearing world.

One of the earliest writers in the twentieth century to chronicle the Broads was W. A. Dutt, a professional journalist who had retired owing to ill health. In 1901, he had published a small book called *Highways & Byways in East Anglia*. This was followed in 1903 by a bigger work entitled simply *The Norfolk Broads*. It was an informed picture of many aspects of the area.

Later, in the 1920s, he would gain a certain notoriety for his embracing the argument for ley lines. As early as 1901, however, he had been intrigued by something that has continued to mystify and haunt the Norfolk coast and Broads for centuries. It was 'Black Shuck'!

Dutt's description is almost Gothic:

> He takes the form of a huge black dog, and prowls along dark lanes and lonesome field footpaths, where, although his howling makes the hearer's blood run cold, his footfalls make no sound. You may know him at once, should you see him, by his fiery eye; he has but one, and that, like the Cyclops', is in the middle of his head. But such an encounter might bring you the worst of luck: it is even said that to meet him is to be warned that your death will occur before the end of the year. So you will do well to shut your eyes if you hear him howling; shut them even if you are uncertain whether it is the dog fiend or the voice of the wind you hear. Should you never set eyes on our Norfolk Snarleyow you may perhaps doubt his existence, and, like other learned folks, tell us that his story is nothing but the old Scandinavian myth of the black hound of Odin, brought to us by the Vikings who long ago settled down on the Norfolk coast.

Was this mysterious and awful hound a direct throwback to the Vikings who had landed in Norfolk so many centuries before?

Or is it simply a myth, exaggerated in the retelling over the years? Whatever the truth is, the fact remains that 'Black Shuck' is talked about to this day. There have even been modern 'sightings'.

Ghosts in Broadland

'Black Shuck' is not the only supernatural mystery of Broadland. The Norfolk Broads have a spookily large population of ghosts. That great landmark in the Broads' history, St Benet's Abbey, has many a story to tell but few more chilling than that of the monk who made a dreadful error of judgement during the Norman occupation. Although an abbey, St Benet's was in effect a fortified castle. Devout as they were, the monks were trained in the use of arms. What's more, the location of the place, surrounded by marshes, made it easy to defend and hard to attack. The point was proven when, having not received an oath of allegiance from the abbot, William, the Norman king, sent an army to show the monks that he was not pleased. After four months, the disciplined and well-trained Norman soldiers had achieved nothing. They could break neither the stronghold nor the spirit of the monks of St Benet's. Retreat to London seemed the only option, but a Norman commander had an idea that he thought might help to avoid disgrace. He suggested to one of the monks, a Brother Veritas, that unnecessary bloodshed was imminent and to avoid it the best plan might be for him to leave the doors unlocked. Payment for such a generous and humane act would be Brother Veritas becoming abbot.

When the doors were left open, at night, the Normans marched in and, aided by the element of surprise and the fact that the monks were asleep, swiftly captured the abbey. Brother Veritas was indeed instantly created abbot. However, in the next instant the Normans hanged him as an example. Treachery was not in their code, even if it had been used to their advantage.

It was 25 May when the misguided monk was killed and many claim that on that night, every year since, the grisly execution can be seen again as ghostly Norman troops hang Brother Veritas from the still-standing bell-tower in the ruins of the abbey.

The Normans left a kindlier haunting at Salhouse, where it's said that a ghostly midnight Mass can be seen. William had given the manor of Salhouse to one of his senior officers, Raoul de Chassagne, Count of Frontagnois. The locals were terrified that this would mean violence and persecution. Nothing was further from the count's mind, apparently, and to show the residents that he intended to protect them he invited them to a midnight Mass by the waterside. Such was the splendour of the occasion that it's repeated, some witnesses say, to this day, the ghostly participants still happy in their peaceful celebration.

Much later, although Britain was still fighting the French, there was the eerie story of two lovers at Potter Heigham. It was just before the Battle of Waterloo and a harsh winter. A young soldier, a drummer, due for active service had fallen in love with a girl from Potter Heigham, but her father did not approve. Perhaps he feared that war would make his daughter a widow, but he was set against her meeting the soldier. They met, as lovers often have, in secret. At a place called Swim Coots the drummer would trudge through the winter weather and skate across the frozen river to meet his sweetheart. That February, though, there had been a sudden rise in temperature and as he skated towards her the ice gave way. He drowned.

They say that in Februaries now, at seven in the evening, the time he died, the soldier, still in uniform and beating his drum to tell her he's coming, can be seen skating forever towards his lost lover.

In another haunting with a specific date, the case of Acle Bridge has continued to be retold and reported. On 7 April it's possible that you'll find a pool of blood on the bridge, a pool that wasn't there the night before.

John Burge was a corn dealer, and not blessed with a good reputation. His tarnished image was not helped when he murdered his wife. He was tried, but when he was acquitted there was much talk of bribery being involved. His dead wife's brother, however, decided to take the law into his own hands.

On 7 April, the brother waited for Burge to return from Great Yarmouth and, meeting him on Acle Bridge, cut his throat. The body lay in a pool of blood. The killer fled to Yarmouth, found a ship and left the country. In his absence another poor wretch was accused, wrongly found guilty and hanged.

Returning to Acle from abroad, Burge's murderous brother-in-law feigned surprise at the events but could not resist visiting the scene of his crime. As he stood on Acle Bridge, on the very anniversary of his killing Burge, he saw a vision in the waters of the river. Was it Burge's ghost? Who knows? But the next morning found the brother-in-law's body hanging from the bridge, dripping blood. The throat had been cut.

And now, on 7 April, on Acle Bridge, a pool of blood appears.

It's in the water that Broadland's most beautiful ghost appears. The 'beautiful Lady of Barton Broad' is an unusual haunting by any standards. It was in the time of the Crusades that this poor young woman was, they say, killed by her father, who accidentally shot her with an arrow. There is a legend that her father had been overseas with the Crusades for years and meeting the girl fell in love with her, not knowing she was his daughter. In a fight with her lover, whom he perceived as a rival, the father shot to kill the other man but hit the girl instead. Only then did he discover her identity and the pointlessness of his amorous feelings. Riddled with guilt, he left for the Holy Land, never to return.

The lovely young woman's face has been seen since, a serene image covering the entire surface of Barton Broad. Quite how earlier sightings of a 'face' covering acres of water were seen from ground level is not known. But, in a strange marriage of ancient legend and new technology, sightings are now claimed – in much more detail, presumably – from low-flying light aircraft.

Like many ghosts of Broadland, the Lady of Barton Broad is very reliable. She appears only on 4 August!

Ghostly black hellhounds and eerie legends were not a deterrent to the growing holiday trade on the Norfolk Broads. It was expanding every year. This was England in its pre-First World War optimism. The Victorian era was gone and now it was as if the Edwardians had created a permanent summer.

Suddenly it was 1908. The Olympics were in London. Sport was on everybody's lips. Football was beginning to develop into the mass interest that would continue to grow, unhindered, for decades. The working class loved it. As for the emerging middle and established upper classes, yachting was the thing.

Let's Go Racing!

If the Victorians had seen the Broads begin to change from a tranquil idyll to a place for fun, the Edwardians continued the process with enthusiasm. It was perhaps at this point that the social and cultural pattern of the Broads began to move into its next stage of development. Yachting and yacht racing had been a part of life on the Norfolk Broads for a long time, and it was the preserve of local people. The origins of organised water sports in the area can obviously be traced back to the great regattas, such as the Thorpe Water Frolics. The Wroxham Regatta was certainly a significant event by the 1890s.

Racing at this time involved all manner of craft, including cruisers and wherries. There is some evidence that a yacht club, for amateurs, but aimed at racing, was formed as early as 1855. It's in 1859, however, that the Norfolk and Suffolk Yacht Club appears. Its emergence is a fascinating snapshot of the changing social pattern. Firstly, the club was founded by a group of seemingly self-styled 'boating gentlemen'. Secondly, despite their genuine enthusiasm for the increasingly popular pastime of racing boats, these gentlemen amateurs wanted a club that drew a line between them and the professional crews.

There was reason for their concern. Yacht crews of full-time 'watermen' had been known to behave badly. There are stories of fights between boats, the craft being lashed together during the fray, redolent of a full naval battle. It would be some time before the 'gentlemen' decided they could sail without the professional crews, though. The first truly amateur trophy was not awarded until 1876.

Dinghy races had become very popular by the 1880s, and it can be argued that the Norfolk Broads were one of the first places to hold them. By then the Yare Sailing Club had been formed, furthering the growth of amateur participation. Regattas and races were held all over the Broads, from Cantley to Horning and Beccles. Such was the geographic spread that the club was renamed the Yare and Bure Yacht Club. An indication of the level of interest is that at one point the Yare and Bure Yacht Club had over 600 members, making it the largest such club in the world.

Different classes of boats were designed and built, with specific races for each of them. The entire business became more and more sophisticated and there were huge debates and differences of opinion over handicaps and rules. It was from this competitive arena that a very special boat would emerge. It was the One Design. The idea was to construct a 'fleet' of identical boats, to make competing fairer. All the craft would be of equal standing. The Royal Norfolk and Suffolk Yacht Club was a powerful body by the turn of the twentieth century, the royal approval itself being a clue to its social standing. In the early 1900s, they commissioned the naval architect Linton Hope to design this new concept of yacht.

Hope, who had several designs to his name and would go on to build flying boats for the Admiralty, came up with a sleek, half-decked boat with a distinctive shape to the bows. Because of the varnished hull, the craft was often called the 'Brown Boat'. Officially, though, this was the 'Broads One Design'. Subsequently, and from other designers, there would be 'Yare and Bure One Design' and by the 1920s the 'Yarmouth One Design'.

Alongside the racing there were commercial activities. The Broads and rivers had changed since the arrival of the railways, but freight was still transported by water and the wherries had not yet disappeared, even if some had been converted to pleasure craft.

One wherry skipper forms an interesting link between these various aspects of pre-First World War life. George Applegate had been born in 1824 and was, by birth, a marsh man. Apparently quite ambitious, he was operating his own wherry, *The Olive*

Branch, when still a young man. He also acquired the lease of Heigham Sounds, which he used for reed cutting. This was a commercially independent but still traditional occupation for a man of his background. Where Applegate was more innovative was that he saw the potential in the boat-hire business. When the railway reached Potter Heigham, George started to hire out boats. He'd stepped out of tradition and in to a new era.

As ever, the railways were happy to drive the market. In 1893, the Great Eastern Railway published their *Summer Holidays in the Land of the Broads*. Their offering cheap return trips was a realistic investment; there were by then over forty boatyards offering hire boats.

If George Applegate is an interesting link between the traditional marsh men and the commercial world of holiday boating, the next serious development in the Broads story is a connection between local Norfolk residents and the new class of 'outsider', or visitor. Ernest Collins was a boatbuilder from Norfolk. He was to meet an accountant from London, a man called Harry Blake.

Collins' father, Robert, had established a boatyard at Wroxham in 1886. The business grew, along with the Broads' own development, and under Ernest became an early success story in building up one of the first really large hire fleets. They also designed and built boats specifically for boating holidays, and were quick to see the opportunities in converting the increasingly commercially unviable wherries to 'wherry yachts' for pleasure cruising. It would not be long before wherries were being built specifically for holidays. Rigged like a wherry, which oozed tradition, but yacht-shaped in the hull, these boats let the holidaymaker be part of 'Broads history' without the need for the skill necessary to sail a wherry. Well equipped for comfort, they usually came with a skipper and a mate to do the work. At the start of the twentieth century, there were over 100 of these boats on the Broads, available from several yards, including Ernest Collins'.

Harry Blake was exactly the sort of young man to hire such a boat. In 1906, he was one of a party of six, from a tennis club in London, who hired a wherry yacht from Ernest Collins. It's sometimes claimed, and is possible, that the boat they took was the *Olive*. What is certain is that Harry and his friends were not impressed with the booking procedure. They had started by asking the railway company for a list of suitable boatyards. They probably went through the increasingly numerous advertisements in the various guides and books that were now so much more available. They found what they wanted, but felt that it had been a bit too much like hard work.

A New Era Begins

The fundamental point is that, having eventually sorted out a boat, they did enjoy the holiday. As their trip drew to a close, Harry Blake realised he'd spotted both the enormous potential and the one weakness in the boat-hire business. It was the selling of the holidays that needed improving. When he got back to Wroxham, he addressed the problem by suggesting that he operate as Ernest Collins' agent, working from London.

In many ways, that was the moment that the modern boat-hire business on the Norfolk Broads began. In truth, it took a little while longer to take shape. Harry Blake did not rush into the venture irresponsibly. He took things a step at a time. Using no more than a pocket diary to record the bookings and transactions, he set about selling holidays for Collins. That first year of 1907 was successful.

Blake's agency really appeared in the following year. Encouraged by the modest success of his 'test marketing', Blake himself started to advertise. It was not a massive campaign like those of decades later; Harry Blake used only one publication, the *Daily Mail*. And the advertisement was a simple classified, running to just three lines. His advertising costs were four shillings and sixpence.

The results proved beyond any doubt that he'd got it right. The advertisement generated over 400 replies. The product was right for the times. By the 1908 season, a Blakes catalogue, the first of many, was in production. About twelve boatyards were listed, offering a total of forty-three yachts for hire. Now there was an agency co-ordinating sales of boating holidays. The holiday 'season' was created, as a period running from May to September, and, establishing a marketing model that remains to this day, there was a catalogue, or brochure, to choose from. There had been some earlier pioneers, but now business on the Broads had changed forever.

1910–1920

The world changed forever a few years later with the outbreak of the First World War. The Edwardian summer of easy days and a peaceful existence was shattered like a mirror.

Although the impact on Norfolk was as dramatic as anywhere, with huge numbers of its men going to war, many never to return, life on the Broads during the First World War was not radically changed. The Blakes catalogue, or 'Yachting List', of 1916 barely makes reference to the fact that there was a war on. It's a book of almost 150 pages, two-thirds of which are details of boats for hire. The company's comments and suggestions give an interesting insight in to the Broads of 1916. With no patriotic statement about the troops abroad or hopes for victory, or peace, it's only in the advertisement for VIX waterproof dressings that there is any hint of the military. The dressings, it's stated, are 'officially supplied to HM military authorities'.

The rest of the advertisements reveal just how big the Broads business had become. Major national brands were now taking space in the catalogue that nine years earlier had been a list of bookings in Harry Blake's pocket diary. Crosse and Blackwell are advertising their brawn, pressed beef and other 'table delicacies', available in tins or glass, and ideal for 'Picnics, Motor and River Parties'. Bird's Custard are eager to point out that 'On the Broads, BIRD'S Custard with Tinned Fruits, Stewed Prunes & c, is appetising and ever-welcome'. Encouragingly, ABDULLA give the reassurance that their cigarettes are 'free from opium'!

Insurance companies and outboard motor manufacturers, whisky and wine sellers, angling magazines and of course the railway all related their products and services to sailing on the Broads.

Perhaps the most ingenious, or tenuous, is that of W. G. Jennings, who was advertising flannel trousers. This London 'Tailor and Breeches Maker' does explain in some detail how his flannels are designed and cut to be eminently suitable for a holiday on the Broads. The extra touch comes in the address: '119 Newgate Street … One minute's walk west of Blakes.'

Undoubtedly the most expected advertiser was, of course, Roys. The business was now centred on Coltishall and Wroxham. They had closed the Dereham shop in 1914 when the manager had been called up for Army service. Trade had been good during the war years, and the peace would see rapid development. But in 1916 their advertising, in the Blakes brochure, speaks volumes about this successful company and its total grasp of the Broads holiday market.

'One minute's walk from the boat houses', 'Goods delivered free to any boatyard or station' and, quite simply, 'Roys of Wroxham provide everything for Yachting and Boating parties' are claims to be taken seriously by the possible holidaymaker. The whole-page advertisement also states that Roys 'take back unopened, any goods left over at the end of cruise and allow in full'. There's also the helpful offer of a 'List of Goods suitable for the trip'. If you don't know what to take, you just have to write to Roys.

Suggestions of what was needed on a Broads boating holiday in 1916 were also offered by Blakes themselves in the front section of their catalogue. Forthright in pointing out that 'the general idea that yachting is a luxury, and that only the well to do indulge in it is quite erroneous, for it is far cheaper than the usual holiday spent at a formal seaside resort, with all its conventionalities', the company also offer a 'stores list', which 'can of course be varied to meet clients' requirements'.

The list was thorough:

Meat (obtained locally)
Bacon (Harris's Wiltshire)
Cooked Hams
Fowls
Sausages (Palethorpe's)
Potted Meats:-
(Crosse and Blackwell's)
Pressed Beef
Pressed Ox Tongue
Oxford Brawn
Chicken and Tongue
Ham and Chicken
Breast of Chicken
Prawns in Aspic
Tea (Twinings)
Coffee
Coffee Essence (Branson's)
Cocoa (Cadbury and Rowntree's)
Milk
Milk Condensed (Nestlé's)
Sugar
Butter
Eggs
Bread
Cake
Jam
Golden Syrup (Lyle's)
'Laitova' Lemon Cheese
Marmalade (Cooper's, Oxford)
Biscuits
'Ufillit' Pastry (Crawford's)
Cheese
Sardines ('Skipper' Brando)
'Sailor' Salmon Slice
Bloater Paste

Potatoes

Vegetables

Fruit

Custard Powder (Bird's)

Flour

'Atora' Beef Suet

Salt ('Cerebos' with pourer)

Mustard

Vinegar

Pepper

Sauce ('Lazenby's')

'L.V.' Pickles

'Bisto' for Gravies

A 'Prana' Sparklet syphon for own mineral water

Ginger Ale

Caley's Cider

'Perrier' Table Water

'Stowers' Lime Juice and Lemon Squash

Domeq's Brandy

Whisky ('Robertsons Yellow Label. Rattray's Hero Brand')

Allsop's Lager

Oxo

Kop's Ale

Candles and Matches

Soap ('Wright's Coal Tar')

'Vim'

Corkscrew and Tin Opener

Oil for Lamp and Stove

'Glosso' Polish for brass work on yacht

Cigarettes

Tobacco

And then came the list of clothing and sundries! Given the extensive 'stores list' it's not surprising that the 'sundries list' is prefaced with the warning not to 'burden yourself with a lot of clothes. Space on a yacht is limited.'

Even so, it's suggested that one needs both 'a best suit and a "Knockabout" one', as well as the following:

Flannel or Drill Trousers
Sweater
Soft Shirts
Collars
Sleeping Apparel
Sun hat and Cap
Stout pair of Boots
Rubber Soled Shoes
Socks
Slippers
Change of Under Clothing
Oilskin or Mackintosh
Towels
Brush and Comb
Torch ('EverReady' recommended)
Vacuum Flask
Portable Meat Safe
Boot Outfit (Chiswick Polish Set recommended)
Tooth Brush
Tooth Paste (Calvert's)
'Auto–Strop' Safety Razor
Shaving Stick (M'Clinton's)
Fishing Tackle
Needles and Cotton
Camera ('Ensignette' recommended)
Muscatol
Pack of Cards, a supply of Magazines, Novels etc.

Muscatol was an insect repellent of the time. The list is rounded off with a recommendation that a 'good fountain pen is indispensable on a cruise for general correspondence, and for use with picture postcards'. The 'Onoto' fountain pen gives absolute satisfaction; also the 'Jewel pen' was highly recommended for your holiday.

These lists are interesting and revealing. Comprehensive and detailed, they reveal that a 'good suit' would not be out of place on an outdoor holiday in 1916. The inference is that sweaters and flannels are the order of the day, with a change into a suit for the evening or excursions. Sufficiently detailed to include shoe-cleaning equipment, the suggestions do not seem to mention any cooking or washing-up materials.

This is almost certainly due to the fact that these holidays were not yet solely 'self-catering'. Skippers and stewards were often part of the package. The arrangements, though, needed explaining:

> As regards boarding the attendants (if taken), the method generally adopted and one which we recommend, is to cater for them yourselves. Another way is to allow them a certain sum a week for their board, say 15/- , and 9*d* a day beer money.

The attendants were, it's explained, 'most obliging' and the 'best of company'. They were a source of 'invaluable advice, especially to the novice', and would take you to 'the most interesting and picturesque parts of the Broads'. There is the overriding impression that all of this information was aimed at a male audience. This notion of the man as the specifier and person booking the holiday would change as roles altered in later years.

To be available for the spring and summer season holidays of 1916, this catalogue would have been designed, written and printed during late 1915, being delivered perhaps after Christmas of that year. It's a pivotal moment. The 'it will be over by Christmas' optimism of 1914 and the early war days was over, but presumably even in late 1915 there was little awareness of the true horror of what lay ahead.

Sociological changes of later in the century aside, the 'gentlemen' to whom the brochure was addressed would soon be gone. Such were the demands of the war that by 1916 conscription was in place. It was no longer a war fought by professional soldiers and volunteers. If you were over eighteen and male, you'd be called.

The pre-conscription men of 1916, however, could still savour Edwardian comforts, in their flannel trousers and 'Knockabout' suits, taking a glass of 'Yellow Label' whisky with their 'Crosse and Blackwell' meats. The unashamed use of brand names within the catalogue was of course an early form of 'product placement', a marketing technique very much in use today. The brands themselves would have been more than happy at these mentions, and happier still that this was in effect not only 'free' advertising, but that it had the added credibility of impartiality.

Blakes were adamant that where brands were mentioned outside of pure advertising, it was because they genuinely recommended the product, and not because advertising had been paid for. They stated it plainly:

> It is solely in the interests of those uninitiated in the catering for such a holiday that attention has been drawn to these firms' specialities and their selection has in no way been influenced by their application for advertising space; indeed, in the interests of our clients we have only accepted instructions from those firms whose goods we can confidently recommend.

It must not be thought that in the pre-TV, pre-Internet age, organisations like Blakes were amateur or primitive marketers. On the contrary, despite the absence of some of the media opportunities of today, these companies were using sophisticated advertising and marketing strategies. The interplay and linkage between the still relatively new Broads boating holiday business and all its possible suppliers is impressive. Food, drink, tobacco, magazines, oil, clothing, insurance and retailers are just some of the industries who had seized the opportunity to promote themselves in publications like the Blakes catalogue, extending their market to a new kind of consumer, or the same consumer in a new kind of environment.

The picture, then, is of a domestic front that is still calm, despite war raging in Europe. On the Broads there are extraordinarily well-provisioned yachts cruising around, guided and steered by attendants and populated by largely male groups of holidaymakers. Blakes had said in the introduction to their catalogue that the Broads holiday was not 'just for the well-off', but a look at the prices of the period suggest that it wasn't for everyone.

A guide to the 'ACTUAL COSTS OF A FORTNIGHT'S CRUISE. PARTY OF SIX GENTLEMEN' gives a suggested budget of £16 for the hire of the boat. Provisions, including all those meats, beers, cigarettes and sundries, plus a tip for the skipper and steward are estimated at £10 10s 0d. Transport from 'home to station and station to home' is given as £3 10s 6d. A price is quoted for 'lunch at the inn' before going on board: a very precise 9s 6d. Another 5s is added for insurance. This made the overall cost of the trip £30 15s 0d, meaning that the cost per head for our six gentlemen was £5 2s 6d for the fortnight, or £2 1s 3d a week. At £2.06 per week it's entertainingly low-cost by any modern standards; but in 1916 the average weekly wage for a fifty-eight-hour week was, depending on the job and the area, under £1. This was a week's holiday that cost twice the weekly income of a working family, at a time when approximately 60 per cent of income was spent on food.

Despite its relatively high cost, and the backdrop of war, the summer of 1916 was an interesting and pleasant time on the Broads. This was a world of fishing and cruising, stopping off at inns, playing a gramophone on the boat during the evening and still feeling part of the great outdoors.

It was at the end of the First World War that the appeal of the Broads fired another literary imagination. Hugh Money-Coutts was not in the first rank of British poets but his account, in verse, of a Broads tour is heartfelt and perceptively detailed about the area. It was published in 1919, as the world adjusted to peace and what, from the viewpoint of the twenty-first century, can be called the years 'between the wars'.

The Norfolk Regiment had sent 32,375 men into the war. They'd fought on the Western Front and in the Middle East, and 5,576 were killed. When the survivors returned, they found things had changed.

The First World War had perhaps not been a cause for concern in the 1916 Yachting Lists of boats for hire but, overseas though it was, the conflict had by then come very close to Broadland. In January 1915, Zeppelin L3 unleashed the first aerial attack on Britain when it bombed Great Yarmouth. For all its mud and trenches, and its antiquated use of horses, the war was also a dreadful catalyst for modernisation. The logistics of the battlefields and trenches had forced into practice many new techniques of excavation and pumping.

Mechanised methods of drainage were among the reason for the disappearance of the marsh men's way of life. By the 1920s, the old existence was all but gone.

Very few wherries were still working as trading boats by 1918. Initially affected by the railways, they were ultimately the victims of road transport. When lorries could carry goods easily and quickly through to Norwich, there was little need for a wherry. The great craft were making the transition from cargo to pleasure cruising. The Broads themselves were becoming more of a playground than a workshop.

Visitor numbers were increasing. Harry Blake, like the pioneers before him, had been proved right. Properly catered-for consumers would prove valuable assets to Norfolk. But local people wanted post-war fun too, and they knew how to enjoy the Broads.

As the wherries evolved, so too did another Norfolk boat. Smaller and less grand, the punt also has an important part in Norfolk Broads history. Shallow of draft and used for all manner of tasks, such as wildfowling, the ancient 'gun punt' would form the basis for a new class of racing boat. The 1920s and 1930s saw yacht racing on the Broads become very popular, and very fast. The Norfolk punt has gone on to be described as one of the most powerful and exciting dinghy classes in the country.

In slower waters, the racing punt's ancestors were a diverse range of local types. The Norfolk Punt is rooted in the Hickling gun punt, from which many a coot was shot. It's the Breydon punt that links together two men who span late nineteenth-century Broadland and much of the twentieth century. Both of them hold unique and special places in Broads history.

Arthur Patterson and Ted Ellis

Arthur Patterson regularly made his way around in his Breydon punt. Born in Great Yarmouth in 1857, Patterson did not have an easy life. He grew up in the Yarmouth Rows, which in the 1850s were not the attractive shopping lanes they are today. They were tough backstreets. Arthur had eight brothers and sisters, and his shoemaker father's income was never enough. With little or no formal education he somehow managed to obtain a string of jobs, including salesman and warehouseman.

Presumably more for genuine self-sufficiency than a hobby, Mr Patterson had an allotment, and it was there that the boy, encouraged by his father, became interested in wildlife. His knowledge was such that he found employment, for a while, as a zookeeper. Ill health and erratic employment were the norm for Patterson until he was in his thirties. He became a truant, or 'school attendance', officer and for the first time in his life found security. It opened the floodgates of creativity. He wrote articles, pamphlets and over twenty-five books, and contributed nature columns to the *Eastern Daily Press* for decades, as 'John Knowlittle'.

His knowledge, skill at natural science and artistic talent allowed him to make a huge contribution to our awareness of the Broads. An expert on fish, he added species to the textbooks. Such was his standing that he was elected as a member of the Linnaean Society.

His 1901 *Catalogue of the Birds of Great Yarmouth* was definitive and hugely respected. And yet, fish and birds aside, one of Patterson's greatest pleasures, and areas of expertise, was the ordinary people of the Broads and Breydon Water. The punt gunners and marsh men were his friends, and often his source of inspiration.

Patterson is a wonderful character in a very 'Norfolk' way. For all his depth and breadth of knowledge, and his being recognised by the scientific institutions, he remains a quiet figure, not catapulted to literary stardom, nor even cult status.

However, he did have a direct influence on someone else who holds a special place in the history of the Norfolk Broads. Ted Ellis was only a boy when he met Arthur Patterson. There are marked similarities in their stories. Neither enjoyed robust health. Both of them achieved academic recognition without having had any formal secondary education, or gaining any recognised qualifications. But both had an all-consuming love of the natural world.

Still in his teens, Ellis got a job at the Castle Museum in Norwich, where he worked as a natural history assistant. He was industrious to say the least, and catalogued flora and fauna with tenacity and accuracy.

Arthur Patterson had encouraged Ted Ellis, and the younger man happily worked with his mentor, assisting him with, among other things, the publication of Patterson's book *Wildfowlers and Poachers*. Ellis also, like Patterson, became a regular writer of newspaper articles and columns. In later years Ted Ellis would become markedly more famous than his friend, and was almost a household name in East Anglia.

Media attention and well-written books were destined to see Ellis remembered, but his real achievement in many ways was that he 'discovered' Wheatfen. Nestled between Surlingham and Rockland Broads, this relatively small area contained such a variety of flora that it was to become a Grade I Site of Special Scientific Interest or SSSI. Ellis' dedicated and painstaking study of the place has contributed enormously to our knowledge of the area's evolution. It was no surprise that Wheatfen became his home in the 1940s.

Again, the contrasts and balances of the Broads come into focus. Away from the quiet of a place like Wheatfen, the Broads were continuing their commercial growth. As the 1930s arrived, so did more marketing activity from the railways.

In 1923, the myriad of small railway companies who had forged the original lines were 'grouped' into four main organisations. The Great Western dominated the West Country and the major routes in and out of it. The London Midland & Scottish Railway, or LMS, had at its core the main lines of the west coast and the Midlands. In the commuter lands and south coast the Southern Railway took control. In the east it was the London & North Eastern Railway, the LNER.

Despite this being perceived as perhaps their 'golden age', the railways had problems. Firstly, after the initial hysteria, there had been little investment for a decade or more, and now the costs of maintenance alone were enormous. Secondly, just like the Norfolk wherries, they were suffering because of competition from road transport.

This they saw as unfair. The argument was that the government were in effect supporting the hauliers by building roads from subsidies imposed on the population. The railways were left to fight their own corner, with fare restrictions making the matter worse. The pressure they put on government had far-reaching consequences, including the introduction of the Vehicle Excise Duty.

In the meantime the railways needed to generate revenue, and they did that by promoting the destinations they could take you to. The Norfolk Broads were ideal. Windmills, ducks, boats and happy holidaymakers appeared in countless posters from the LNER, all of them clearly stating 'NORFOLK BROADS' and 'IT'S QUICKER BY RAIL'. The quality of the artwork was outstanding, and completely in keeping with the style of the time.

All of the pictures, in their different ways, convey the same messages. The Norfolk Broads are the place to go, and the railway is how to get there. As stunning and effective as these campaigns were, they could not be seen as truly innovative. The old independent railway companies had initiated the approach much earlier. The Great Eastern had, after all, commissioned high-quality photographs to advertise the Broads, albeit tacitly, in their carriages back in the 1880s.

But now there was a more powerful advertising machine driving trade towards Norfolk. On the Broads, the power cruiser had arrived.

1920–1945

In many ways the emergence of this type of boat was inevitable. It suited the times. Norfolk boatyards were building more of them to meet customer demand, and, as the sole 'big player' of the time, Blakes was increasing the number of power cruisers for hire. By 1930, the brochure had over seventy pages of them.

They came in all sizes, some as big as 60 feet long. This was the era of the picnic hamper and the gramophone. It was interwar Britain having fun. And now it was affordable fun. In fact, demand and volume meant that some prices for a fortnight's holiday on the Broads had reduced since a decade earlier. A cost of £8 a week for a small boat out of Brundall was less than the average price that Blakes had been quoting in 1920.

There's little doubt that the boatyards and the Blakes agency had a sense of nervousness about inexperienced 'sailors' taking off on the Broads in powered boats. Many of the brochures and advertisements of the time underline the idea of taking out insurance. This had been offered in the 1916 brochure, but now there are suggestions as to the size of boat one hired, relating it to the amount experience you had.

The price structure was also taking shape. What can be seen evolving is a business model that would become part of modern holiday marketing. The time of year had a direct relation to the cost of hire.

As had happened before in the unfolding story of the Broads, when all of this commerce and activity was reaching its height, on to the stage stepped an observer who would take a different view.

In the past there had been the contrasts between the 'staged' photographs and the natural ones. The painters of the Norwich

School had sought to capture a quaint atmosphere, to have it balanced by writers and observers who saw the real hardship of reed cutting and river work. Now came Arthur Ransome. He would make the Broads as attractive as ever. He would also highlight the social distinctions between those who worked and played there.

Arthur Ransome

Ransome was born in 1884. He had published some books on nature, for children, as early as 1906, but had gone on to write biographies, including one of Oscar Wilde that had resulted in a court case.

Just before the First World War he had moved to Russia, from where he published a book of folk tales. His first marriage had collapsed and while in Russia he met his second wife, who was working as a secretary to Trotsky.

The next few years were colourful to say the least. Ransome found himself embroiled in espionage and diplomatic errands. When the dust was settling on the Russian Revolution, during which his loyalty to Britain was questioned, he stayed in the Baltic. It was there that he built a cruising yacht for himself and wrote a book about it called *Racundra's First Cruise*. Perhaps this was the first indication of what would draw him to the Broads. Certainly rustic life appealed to him, and as a staff member for *The Guardian* he wrote the Country Diary column.

Once back in England he set up home in the Lake District and it was there, in 1929, that he wrote *Swallows and Amazons*. The novel would give its name to a series of books and ensure Ransome's reputation as a fine writer. These books were aimed at children but their quality was such that they neither patronised the younger reader nor failed to satisfy a more mature audience. They were tales of adventure, set in the Lake District, and they painted pictures of a life that children would love, and adults wished they'd had.

It was the fifth book in the series, *Coot Club*, published in 1934, that was the first to be set on the Norfolk Broads. Ransome had visited Norfolk, and the Broads appealed to him. It's noticeable that in his Lake District books the locations are fictional recreations of real places. The various activities of the characters are described in authentic detail, but the places cannot really be identified. However, in the Norfolk books he used real places; *Coot Club* is very specific about its Horning setting.

Ransome's skill was certainly acknowledged by the critics. Perhaps literary pundits of the 1930s were not in the swelling ranks of Broads visitors, though. It's a positive review, but the critic from *The Guardian* still plainly felt that the Broads were off the beaten track. He wrote,

> There is a satisfactory realism about all that happens to the Coot Club, and the atmosphere and detail of the odd part of England where they navigate are conveyed with a charm and accuracy that only this author perhaps could bring to bear.

Coot Club opens at Thorpe station, in Norwich. Within a matter of a few sentences Ransome describes exactly how and where the terminus fits in to the Norfolk railway network, with trains from the south running out the same way they came in if they are bound for places like Wroxham.

The geographical context of the book is so embracing that the end papers are maps of the northern and southern Broads. At the appropriate point in the story there is a note from the author to explain that if readers want to know where they are from there on, it's time to refer to the other map.

Wroxham, Beccles and Horning are all featured, and yachts like the *Titmouse* and *Teasel* are accurately described; indeed, drawings are included.

From the first meeting of the young characters it's obvious that there is a difference between local Broads residents and visitors. However, not all visitors are 'bad'. The Callum children, spending their Easter holidays in Norfolk, soon get on with the local youngsters. There is a shared passion for all things boating. Trouble arrives when other visitors pose a threat to a nesting site that the Coot Club have taken it upon themselves to protect.

The 'other visitors' are therefore the villains of the piece. Symbols of their villainy, almost worse than nest wrecking, are the fact that they have hired a motor cruiser, and that they make a lot of noise. They are referred to as the 'Hullabaloos'!

When young Tom, of the Coot Club, takes some action against these selfish intruders, the lady with whom the Callum children are staying promises not to give him away. But she has a price. Worth far more than money, and much more worthy than any material possessions of the 'Hullabaloos', her price is that Horning lad Tom teaches the Callum kids to sail.

While all of this is set against a brilliantly painted backdrop of Norfolk, and laced with wonderful detail, there is a real feeling of division throughout the book. Despite their different origins, the children all represent conservation, old values, and sailing. The 'Hullabaloos' are from the city; they are noisy and modern. And they have a motor cruiser.

Ransome had nailed his colours to the mast. Yachts have masts. Motor cruisers don't.

There is strange resonance about the timing of this story. Nobody could deny the importance of the trade that the ever increasing holiday business was bringing to Norfolk. And yet, not for the first time even then, there were emerging signs of the divergence between conservation and recreation.

During the 1920s and 1930s, as trains got faster, and indeed the boats got speedier, there was another challenge to be the 'fastest' in Broadland. It came in the form of 'Billy Bluelight', a true character in the history of the region.

Billy, whose real name was William Cullum, was born in Norwich in 1859. Details of his life are sketchy, but it's generally assumed that he lived with his mother in the Oak Street area of the city, at least until she died in the 1930s.

It's known that he worked for a time in the legendary Caley's chocolate factory in Norwich, but he was also a street trader. One theory regarding his nickname is that it comes from the blue-tipped matches he sold along with flowers. He would stand near the

Royal Arcade in Norwich attracting custom with imaginative sales patter.

It's also possible that the name 'Bluelight' was a reference to his lifestyle. A teetotaller, he would evangelise against the dangers of drink to anybody who would listen, often delivering unsolicited 'lectures' outside pubs and factory gates. In Victorian slang an abstainer was often referred to as a 'Bluelight'.

His clean, albeit itinerant, habits presumably accounted for his famous athleticism. Billy's place in history is enshrined in his famous racing against the boats. The peak of his fame was during the interwar years.

Quite simply, he would challenge boats to a race. He would take on all comers, from wherries, who were still plying their commercial trade and could move very quickly, to pleasure craft. He would have proved an interesting sight, especially for holidaymakers and trippers. With a striped cricket cap on his head and wearing long running shorts, he also wore a white vest emblazoned with medals. The provenance of these decorations is not known. From the riverbank, usually at Bramerton, he would shout out his challenge,

My name is Billy Bluelight,
my age is 45,
I hope to get to Carrow Bridge
before the boat arrive.

And that's what he did. Dashing off along the bank he would run across the common land, through Whitlingham, and appear at Crown Point, where he could be seen by the people on the boat he'd challenged.

With a theatrical flourish he would then disappear, running over to Trowse, where he crossed the bridge. This would mean that he could get to Carrow Bridge, on the edge of Norwich, in time to be there when the boat arrived. People loved him for it. There would be applause, and money would be thrown at him.

Billy's challenge never changed, so it would appear that he stayed at the age of forty-five for some considerable time.

As the 1930s slipped by, there were perhaps echoes of the pre-First World War tranquillity. Certainly the enthusiasm for Broads holidays continued to grow. Fuelled by transport, advertising and the chance for people to have some leisure time, the numbers grew each year.

If the Edwardian peace had been shattered by the first great war in Europe, the 1930s would end as the world once more exploded in to conflict. In 1939, there were over 100,000 holidaymakers on the Norfolk Broads. Life would change instantly in September that year with the outbreak of the Second World War.

The Second World War

Great Yarmouth being bombed was the nearest the war had come to Broadland in the First World War. The population had changed as men went to fight, but it was not here that the battles were waged. Now there was a new warfare. Air raids and civilian casualties brought the horror of it to the home front. Suddenly, holidays were not just further down people's priority lists, they were in a very real sense not possible.

Initially, it was impossible to predict how the war would develop. Certainly nobody in 1939 could have foreseen the enormity of the next six years.

The Blakes brochure for 1940 has been referred to as the 'brochure that never was'. Produced in 1939 for the 1940 season, it could never have been distributed so widely, nor obtained as many bookings, as its recent predecessors.

Its contents speak volumes.

The front cover, emblazoned with the flags of participating boatyards, proudly announces, 'NORFOLK BROADS HOLIDAYS AFLOAT: THE HOLIDAY THAT IS DIFFERENT.' But immediately below that headline the tone changes. There is no idyllic sailing scene. In simple type, the front cover is given over to some practicalities.

Owing to the rationing of paper, it's explained, the company have tried to help by printing the brochure in three sections: Editorial, Yachts and Motor Cruisers.

The Motor Cruisers section contained the houseboats on the Broads and the 'craft on the Cam and Ouse'. The idea was that clients interested in yachts would need only the Yachts and Editorial sections, and likewise for those wanting a motor cruiser. There was an optimistic caveat: 'Of course any client may have the three sections on request.'

Inside the brochure, the introductory page is interesting.

Firstly, like the front cover, it made clear that this was the brochure from *Norfolk Broads Holidays Afloat*. The purely Blakes branding, evident as early as the 1916 catalogue, had gone. Rather this is Blake's Limited, making the point that they are 'the central booking office for all members of the Norfolk and Suffolk Broads Yacht Owners Association'.

This position is amplified in the declaration that 'thirty-three years ago we were appointed as the Sole Representatives of the Yacht Owners and today are proud to still hold that office'.

There was still only a London address, in Newgate Street. Blake's obviously expected customers to visit, as, aside from the address itself, there are references to the office being near St Paul's tube station, and a suggestion to 'LOOK FOR OUR CLOCK'. It's only in relatively small type, under the main headline, that we read that this is 'the War Edition' of the brochure.

Overleaf, and over Harry Blake's signature, the realities of the national predicament were brought into focus. The terms for 1940 were to be held at 1939 prices for as long as possible, although it was made plain that costs were rising.

Under the frankly chilling sub headline of 'WAR RISKS' it was explained that, to help clients during wartime, contracts could be cancelled by either party if warranted by war risks only, and the deposit would be refunded in full.

As to rationing, Blake's were still awaiting official information on the quantity of petrol that would be allowed, although they had 'been assured' that a 'supply sufficient for cruising in moderation would be forthcoming'. Regarding food, there was a promise that the company were doing their best 'to enable clients to obtain those articles which are rationed as easily as possible'.

The production of the brochure had presumably meant that the sections had been printed at different times as these stark but realistic warnings on rationing are not evident in any of the advertising for food and drink.

Roys of Wroxham's advertisement appeared on the inside front cover, offering an abundance of wines, beers, fish, fruit, vegetables, bread, milk, tobacco and all manner of fishing tackle, gramophones and cameras. The outside back cover carried a full-colour advertisement for 'BRAND'S DELICACIES' to ensure that you would be able to produce 'appetising, satisfying, "ready to serve" meals just whenever you want them'. And it was all available from Roys of Wroxham.

Just as Blakes were the sole booking agents for the Yacht Owners Association, Thomas Cook had established themselves as the sole travel agents for Blakes. Operating from a central base in Berkeley Street, London, and a network of provincial offices, Cook would organise your train journey to the Broads, and Blakes in particular.

The infrastructure of marketing was in full swing by this time but events were to overtake the advertisers of 1940. Rationing would arrive and last for a long time. Food shortages would be commonplace. As for travel, there would be new limitations. Soon a new style of advertising would emerge. Government posters would issue warnings over secrecy and the need for prudence. 'NORFOLK BROADS HOLIDAYS AFLOAT: THE HOLIDAY THAT IS DIFFERENT' would soon be competing with 'Is your journey really necessary?'

For all the guarded optimism of late 1939, and the release of the 'War Edition' brochure, the Broads holiday industry was brought to a juddering halt in June 1940.

With invasion by Germany a real threat, and security at its highest, the Broads were seen as a vulnerable chink in the nation's armour. They were in effect shut down.

Some of the measures taken were dramatic. Fearful of enemy troops being brought in by seaplane, the government authorised blockades. On some stretches of water these were made from local boats, requisitioned from both private and boatyard ownership. The craft were often sunk to create obstacles and reduce access. Many a Broads boat, including some wherries, ended their days by defending the realm in this way.

Necessity being the mother of invention, there now sprung up a new relationship. With a war to fight, the government needed more boats. With holidays not on the agenda, Broadland boatyards needed work. Almost inevitably, the craftsmen of Norfolk began building boats for the war effort. Woods, Brooms and Powell's were just three of the Broads yards that built for the government.

These were strange times on the Broads. It would have been possible to see a motor cruiser that a year earlier would have been the joy of someone's holiday, patrolling the rivers with a mounted machine gun. Certainly some of the Broom boats saw service in this way, and as billets for troops. Another sighting could well have been a landing craft. Now enshrined in history as the great barges that took troops to the Normandy beaches on D-Day, some of these were built and tested on the Norfolk Broads.

Other wartime building projects included motor cruisers adapted for minelaying. Bigger craft were commissioned as well, bringing certain logistical challenges with them. Some of these ships were built on the northern rivers of the Broads, and the problems arose when they proved too big for Acle Bridge. Plans were put in place to put the superstructures together in a temporary yard at Great Yarmouth. In a stark reminder of how close modern warfare was to the home front, the yard was destroyed by enemy action. With the resourcefulness born of wartime needs, the work was moved around the yards, while daily lorry runs ferried staff around to do it.

These darkest of days drew all of the effort available into the war. Activity on the Broads was, as it was everywhere, concentrated on defending the country against invasion. But, as warships were built and boats were sunk as blockades, much of the pre-war hire fleets simply lay moored, gathering dust and going without maintenance.

Something approaching normality began to reappear on the Broads before the war was over. Even before the watershed D-Day landings of 1944, there had been a marked decrease in the fear of invasion. Some of the earlier controls had been removed by 1943, resulting in a noticeable return of holidaymakers to the Broads. It wasn't of course anything approaching the visitor numbers of the mid-1930s. But then, in another of those twists of history, there would not have been enough capacity to deal with that volume anyway. It was going to take time to service, repair and refurbish the boats that had survived, but sat still, for the last three years.

Another social effect of the war was the movement of evacuees. Children had been sent away from the increased danger of living in the cities likely to be bombed. Later, families who had lost their homes in air raids would be billeted outside the bigger conurbations. Some of the London families were despatched to East Anglia. During 1944, the harbour master at Oulton Broad was involved in finding them billets on motor cruisers, moored to serve as houseboats. He brokered these arrangements on behalf of the boat owners.

The harbour master would become more and more involved with boat hire. His name was Hoseason.

The period immediately following the end of the Second World War inevitably brought changes to all walks of life. The cataclysmic effect of six years of war had touched, in some way or another, every family, and every business, in Britain. It was a time to rebuild, plan ahead and prepare for the future. In the history of the Norfolk Broads, embracing as it does the pursuits of families and the world of commerce, it was a pivotal time.

To begin with, the fleets that had lain idle needed to be refurbished and brought up to the specification needed for customers to hire.

While Broadland had not been punished by bombing in the way that cities had been pounded, the long period of commercial inactivity mixed with wartime security measures meant that the Broads, and the boats, were in disarray. The anti-invasion tactics of sinking boats to make blockades may not have been needed to fend off German soldiers, but now they made the Broads dangerous, in places, for the unskilled sailor. What's more, petrol was still rationed, which meant that powered cruising was not seen as a necessity by a government trying to make do with scant resources.

And yet, there is reason to believe that this was a turning point in the fortunes of the Broads. The old life, already altered by First World War, was now changed forever. The marsh men were all but an extinct race. Agriculture was embracing the tractor and powered machinery, leaving behind the traditions of horse working. A new life was emerging, and it brought visitors. The village gatherings and regattas carried on, but the motor cruiser, and holidaying on it, had arrived.

In this time of change, two legendary names would change their status forever. Harry Blake was sixty-five in 1945, and he retired. The agency, which had been his idea and indeed became 'his' business, was sold. The interesting point is that it was bought by a group of the boatyard, and craft, owners he had represented. It was a timely, and telling, transition. Created by a London-based visitor to the Broads who had seen, and realised, the potential in organising and promoting holidays on the Broads, the agency he had built was moving back in to the control of local businesspeople who felt it was time that they had more of a say in how their lettings were organised.

The clue was in the name change. Now the company would be called Blakes (Norfolk Broads Holidays) Ltd. It was the first step in a journey that, just under twenty years later, would see the head office move from London to Wroxham.

The year 1946 saw Blakes with a new name, a new – albeit 'austerity'-quality – brochure and a new general manager. It also had a new competitor.

6

The Second Half of the Twentieth Century

1945–1960

Hoseasons Arrives on the Broads

At just four pages, the first Hoseasons 'brochure' did not appear to be much of a challenge to even the reduced-quality Blakes publication of that year. But Wally Hoseason, the harbour master who, like Harry Blake before him, had seen an opportunity on the Broads, had arrived.

Enthused by the original idea he'd had while organising wartime billets, W. B. 'Wally' Hoseason had soon extended his Oulton boatyard into the business of hiring cruisers for recreation. He'd given up his post as harbour master to launch his venture as early as 1944. By 1945, hiring had already overtaken boatbuilding as the firm's main activity. As Blakes regrouped itself for a post-war era of prosperous holiday business, so Wally Hoseason began to expand his empire to meet the same ambitions.

It was a tiny brochure in 1946, but he had sold 200 holidays the previous year and he now set his sights on a wider geographic spread.

For the emerging post-war holidaymakers there was now a choice of two 'big' names. Aside from the myriad of independent boatyards who rented out boats, there was the option of choosing from the now long-established, but recently reorganised, Blakes or the much newer, but plainly growing, agency with the odd name: Hoseasons. People wondered; was it a contraction of holiday seasons? What did it mean? The truth was that it was simply a surname, like Blake.

William Ballantyne Hoseason had been born a Shetlander in 1887. He'd left an early farming life to take the harbour master post at Oulton in the 1930s, and the contacts he made in that role served him well as he developed his business. He'd married, and he and his wife Jessie had a son, James, born in 1927.

James, or Jimmy, Hoseason was a pupil at Lowestoft Grammar School during the war. He had a brief spell teaching maths when he left, but simultaneously studied civil engineering at night school. Qualified, he moved to London to work for McAlpine and start his career. It was not to be. In 1949, his father contracted tuberculosis and Jimmy moved back to Suffolk to help at the boatyard. Wally died in 1950. Jimmy took over the business.

Neither of the original founders were in control, but the Broads now had two businesses that would define the following decades: Blakes and Hoseasons.

With two key players in place, and a growing awareness of marketing and media opportunities, the 1950s would see significant commercial and social changes that contributed greatly to the development of the future of Broads as a holiday destination. But this was also the decade when the past of these unique Norfolk waterways would come into focus in a way that would challenge their very origins.

How the Broads Came to Be: Dr Joyce Lambert
Dr Joyce Lambert had been born in London in 1916. She was to begin her association with the Broads quite early in her life when her family moved to Norfolk. She grew up in Broadland, at Brundall. She went to the Norwich High School for Girls before obtaining her degree in Botany from University College of Wales, Aberystwyth, at the outbreak of war in 1939. Returning to Norwich briefly for a

teaching post, she moved on to become a lecturer in Botany at what was then Westfield College within the University of London.

Her first area of research was not the Broads, but the Fens. By 1946, she was publishing academic work on their ecology. Two years later she moved again, to the University of Cambridge, where she shifted her area of study to the Fens and Broads of the River Bure.

A colleague of hers at the time named J. N. Jennings was also studying the Broads – Joyce and Jennings published papers together in the *Journal of Ecology* in 1951. Then, in 1952, he published his book, *The Origins of the Broads*. In it he claimed that, while there might be exceptions, the Broads were a natural phenomenon.

Jennings had not reckoned for the startling challenge to his claims that would come from Joyce Lambert. In her studies she had used a different technique. She had been working on plants in the peat deposits and had carried out tests, encouraged by that devotee of the Broads Ted Ellis. Around Surlingham Broad she made several borings into the peat, smaller than those used by Jennings. Her results were sufficiently intriguing for her to make hundreds more borings, across a wider area. The outcomes were always the same, and impossible to ignore.

Beneath the mud, the peat-lined bottoms of the Broads were unnaturally flat and even. What's more, the sides were uncannily vertical. Adding even more intrigue was the fact that the Broads often contained islands of peat. And they had vertical sides too. There were also pathways of peat, which not only ran in clearly defined parallel lines but also adhered to the land boundaries that could still be seen on early maps.

The evidence was irresistible. The Broads were peat diggings. They were man-made.

Lambert was due to deliver the presidential address for the Norfolk and Norwich Naturalists' Society in 1952 and intended to publish the speech. It was when she was preparing it for publication, in the final editing stage, that she included references to her discoveries. She subsequently published a further article in the *Geographical Journal*.

From a twenty-first-century viewpoint, informed of the history of Roman Britain, and the continued use of peat as a fuel by the Normans, it's difficult to understand the impact of Joyce Lambert's discovery. Often in valleys and to the side of the main rivers, muddied by centuries of slow change, the question of the Broads origins had simply fallen from memory and debate. Suddenly it was very much back in the spotlight. As is often the case with breakthrough revelations, Lambert's work created an instant sensation, quickly followed by more questions.

If the Broads were man-made, how could such an extensive excavation have been achieved, by hand, in what had been, and still was, a floodplain?

Scientists and historians worked together to rediscover the Broads and uncover their early history. The University of Cambridge was instrumental in drawing together the work and the findings. There was extensive re-examination of ancient documents, confirming the vast extraction of peat as a fuel in the twelfth century. With that came the scientific evidence that not only had digging taken place much earlier, but that great skill and knowledge had been employed. Tests showed that the long-forgotten workers had dug deep. The reason was commercial and pragmatic: peat at 2–3 metres below the surface was better fuel than that near the surface.

The relevance of the lines that followed man-made, and mapped, boundaries was also confirmed. Joyce had been right. History showed that individual parishes had had the right to excavate peat in their own territories, which had been clearly defined. They matched the findings.

Joyce Lambert's grandfather had built a house in the Yare Valley during the 1920s. It was to there that she retired in 1979. She'd never married, and as she became frailer she needed the care of a nursing home, where she spent the last three years of her life. She died there in May 2005.

It's impossible to overstate her place in the history of the Norfolk Broads.

While the academic world busied itself with the newly rewritten history of the Broads' origins, the general public was looking to what they might hold for the future. This was post-war Britain, and for all the shortages and rationing there was an optimism. It was the era of the Festival of Britain, the coronation of a new queen, Everest conquered and the safety of peace. Not all of the pre-war attitudes and conventions were gone, but there was a new democracy and social mobility. Consumerism was beginning to flex its muscles, and holidays were something more people wanted, and could achieve.

In Lowestoft, James Hoseason was considering his future. He was running his late father's business, and seriously considering selling it. Blakes was now operating in its newer form, with more of the control in the hands of the owners. It was a strong and successful co-operative business. It was also, in reality, still run from London.

Hoseason recognised that there was therefore room for a competitor based on a different business model. He believed that a private company could market boating holidays on behalf of owners too. He also believed that such a company, locally based, would be more efficient in managing the fleet. He decided not to sell, but to expand.

By 1952, Hoseasons was not only selling holidays on boats, it was hiring out riverside properties. Anglers were an important audience in the newly emerging marketing mix. Two years later the company took another important step when it bought the Thurman booking agency in Potter Heigham.

There were of course dozens of boatyards looking after their own lettings, including the legendary Herbert Woods. Indeed there was another agency, Bradbeers, who had been operating from Lowestoft since 1948. Sailing and yacht clubs were still popular, but as far as holidays were concerned the motor cruiser was making serious inroads.

By 1951, the Blakes listings had ten pages more of motor cruisers than it did yachts. In 1953, by which time he was representing some twelve boatyards, compared to Blakes' thirty-two, Hoseason was listing three times as many motor cruisers as sailing craft. By this time Hoseason was also showing page after page of houseboats, houses, bungalows and caravans.

The Blakes operation was not falling behind the relative newcomer in marketing techniques however. Flexible payment plans had been introduced, fitting precisely with the emerging 'hire-purchase' arrangements that were helping to satisfy consumers' desires to 'have it now'. Blakes also sent every customer a copy of their booklet of handy hints for boating holidays, *Anchors Aweigh*.

This pocket-sized book had been around since the 1940s, when its cover was almost official in its blandness. By the 1950s, the graphics were very much of their time. The 1950 edition wastes no time in dealing with the rationing question on its first inside page. There are clear instructions on how to order food, reminding customers that they will need to present their ration books on arrival.

Tellingly, the first 'Rule of The River' given in the booklet is 'All craft under power should keep out of the way of sailing vessels'. That was not 'give way to'; it was 'keep out of the way of'.

There were tide tables and regatta dates, nautical terms and hints on mooring. Local early closing days were listed and there were maps and directions. It was a commendable communication with customers, even if the language is a little formal by modern standards.

Towards the back of the book, however, is a particularly interesting article. It's a 'Message from the Broadland Protection Society' under the chairmanship of Herbert Woods. The message is clear. Many visitors, 'and others,' it said, feel that they would like to assist in the preservation of 'these waterways ... Almost every owner of hire craft contributes towards safeguarding public navigational rights, and the clearance of weeds and reeds which are reducing the amount of open water available to both the sailing enthusiast and the cruising man alike.'

The article pointed out that during 1949 the society had cleared some 60 acres of Barton Broad and that the work had been made possible because the society, and the Norfolk and Suffolk Broads

Yacht Owners Association had acquired a mechanical weed cutter for the purpose. In the same year, it stated, the society had successfully obtained summer access to Hoveton Little Broad, meaning that in all some 110 acres of water had been opened up to sailors and holidaymakers.

There was then a request for donations as 'more can be done if all holidaymakers associate with the boat owners in contributing generously to this extremely useful work'. Donations could be made on taking over your boat, or posted to Blakes' London office.

This is an interesting insight in to the spirit of the times. Once again it's possible to see the contrasts and balances that recur throughout Broads history. It's plain that there was still a significant perceived difference between the sailor and the 'cruising man'. There was an obvious love of the Broads and spots like 'that most delightful stretch of water known as Hoveton Little Broad', but, for all that there was a hint of 'preservation' in the article, the reality is that this was not about protecting the natural habitat; it was about opening up more of the Broads to sailing and cruising. And it was asking for donations to help do it.

Voluntary work and donations were also sought by those with a less commercial and more specifically conservation-driven agenda. As far as the Broads are concerned, it's at this point that the vexed question of National Park status comes into the story.

The National Park Question

Increasing awareness of the deterioration of the natural landscape, together with a grudging acceptance of little or no governmental contribution, had galvanised people in to voluntary action as far back as 1888. The Breydon Wild Birds Protection Society had been formed then to help enforce the Wild Birds Protection Act and reduce the large-scale shooting of rare birds on Breydon Water. Norfolk was a pioneering region in the establishment of county trusts with the formation of the Norfolk Naturalists Trust.

But it was in the years after the Second World War that the issue of National Parks, and how it related to the Norfolk Broads, really started to develop. The perennial debate of commercial land usage, including agriculture and tourism, bringing as it does income and prosperity, versus the conservation of the environment, was not unique to the Broads. All over the country the same scales were constantly weighed.

Bowing to pressure from several groups, a committee was formed, under the leadership of the then Parliamentary Secretary to the Minister of Agriculture, Christopher Addison. By 1931, their report had recommended the formation of a National Parks scheme. Such were the national conditions that the proposals went nowhere, swamped by concerns over the Depression and the financial climate.

And yet, with all the worries of the war raging around them, the 1940s government was attentive to the idea of National Parks and their role in a post-war world. In 1941, Lord Justice Scott chaired a committee to discuss the question of rural development and its report came out in favour of National Parks. The recommendation contained some pivotal words in the weighing of priorities. 'Existing land usage,' it said, quoting agriculture as an example, 'should be continued, but be secondary to the main purpose which is public recreation.' The issue of conservation was to be addressed by the separate concept of Nature Reserves, which could be inside, or outside, of National Parks.

It's later that a working definition of a National Park began to emerge. It came from the Ministry of Town and Country Planning, who had been asked by the wartime government to develop thinking in the light of Lord Justice Scott's work.

Several important definitions and objectives were set down, including the overarching description as 'an extensive area of beautiful and relatively wild country'.

The National Parks would aim, it said, to be areas in which the characteristic landscape beauty is strictly preserved, access and facilities for public open-air enjoyment are simply provided, wildlife, and buildings and places of architectural and historic interest are suitably protected, and yet established farming use is effectively maintained.

Before looking at how this definition affected the Broads, and what happened next, it's worth pausing for a moment to consider several points. Firstly, history has tended to overlook that as early as the 1930s there had been a direct proposal, from a Dr Cornish, that the Broads become a National Park. Secondly, all of this work and debate was going on prior to Joyce Lambert's work. As informed and strategic as the discussions were, they were in ignorance of the origins of the Broads. Also, nobody involved, from Lord Justice Scott to John Dower, who headed up the Ministry of Town and Country Planning team, accurately foresaw or predicted the growth in road transport, tourism and social mobility that would radically alter their vision of post-war life.

John Dower's team had completed their report by the end of the war. It did not bode well for the Broads. He saw the already developed holiday industry sitting alongside the intensive agriculture of the area as an uneasy fit with his vision of a National Park as 'wild uplands'. It all looked like too much hard work. The complications of drainage and navigation meant it was not like other candidate areas.

Norfolk has always prided itself, and always will, on being 'different'. At this point, its differences were doing the county no favours. The best Dower could offer was to put the Broads on a 'reserve list', and float the idea that it should be dealt with in some 'ad hoc scheme of local and national action'.

Opinion and recommendation would continue to ebb and flow for years. The Hobhouse Report of 1947 was much more encouraging for Broadland. Waxing uncharacteristically lyrical for a government document, this initially suggested that the Broads were 'a potential National Park which seems to belong to another world, so widely does it differ from the mountains and wild moorlands of the north and west'.

This complete about face from John Dower's concerns was followed by Hobhouse pointing out, in a phrase that strikes a chord to resonate throughout this entire story, that 'the Broads have a special claim to selection as a National Park quite apart from their

1. *On the Norfolk Broads*, Henry Bright, *c.* 1855. (Yale Center for British Art, Paul Mellon Collection)

2. *St Benet's Abbey*, attributed to John Sell Cotman, *c.* 1810. (Yale Center for British Art, bequest of Richard L. Purdy)

3. *The Norfolk Broads*, John Sell Cotman, undated. (Yale Center for British Art, Paul Mellon Collection)

4. *Gathering Water Lilies*, P. H. Emerson, 1886. (Library of Congress)

5. *The Old Order and the New*, P. H. Emerson, 1886. (Library of Congress)

6. *Ricking the Reed*, P. H. Emerson, 1886. (Library of Congress)

7. *Quanting the Marsh Hay, Norfolk Broads, England*, P. H. Emerson, 1886. (Library of Congress)

8. *Poling the Marsh Hay*, P. H. Emerson, 1886. (Library of Congress)

Top: 9. Traditional and modern boats on the River Bure. (Picture courtesy of Broads Authority)

Middle: 10. The Blakes Yachting List of 1916. The design is redolent of the era, and the classic Broads scene had already made its way into promotional material. In almost 150 pages, two-thirds of which are details of boats for hire, the catalogue barely mentions the fact that there is a war in progress.

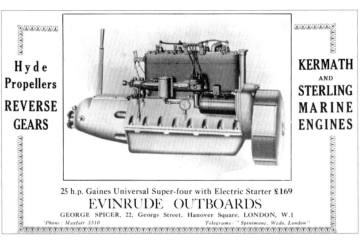

Bottom: 11. 1920s technology at its finest: the Evinrude Outboard, £169 worth of power.

Right: 12. Blake's advertising in 1927: an average of £4 per head per week. 'You only have to enjoy yourself.'

Below: 13. 1940s power from Gray Engines. Now the message is all about ease and economy, with no mention of the price. Engine manufacturers had regularly advertised in what were primarily holiday publications. It was a way of reaching the boating enthusiast, and being seen to support the fleets that used their products.

Norfolk Broads Holidays

THE NORFOLK BROADS, with their natural beauties and quiet old-world villages, will enchant you. They are 120 miles from London, and consist of 200 miles of safe inland rivers and lakes, situated between Cromer, Lowestoft and the fine old city of Norwich, with its Cathedral and Castle. You hire from us for a week or longer a fully furnished wherry, yacht or motor boat, which becomes your floating home, moving when and where you wish, inland, not on the sea. We can supply an attendant to manage the boat and do all cooking. You only have to enjoy yourself. The cost, including boat, food, etc., averages £4 per head per week.

FREE 212-page booklet containing details of 200 yachts, wherries, motor boats, camping skiffs, houseboats, bungalows to hire or for hire, and long article : "How to enjoy a Broads Holiday." Apply for copy at once.

Train Services, Fares and other information, from any L.N.E.R. Enquiry Office.

BLAKE'S 7, BROADLAND HOUSE, 22, NEWGATE ST., LONDON E.C.1

EASY TO INSTALL
MORE POWER • LESS FUEL

Power, Reliability, Smooth-running, Economy—every Gray owner will tell you that these are the outstanding characteristics of these trusty engines. Models from 9 to 160 h.p., 4, 6, and 8 cylinders, for auxiliaries, launches, cruisers.

★ **GRAY "FOUR-40"** (illustrated below) ★
Unbeatable for economy. The Gray exclusive INDIVIDUAL PORTING design gives nearest approach to 6-cylinder smoothness.

GRAY DIESELS. Proved design, with 10 million miles tested service on land and sea. Five models: 1, 2, 3, 4 and 6 cylinders.

ASSOCIATED MANUFACTURERS Co. (LONDON) Ltd.
Palace of Industry, Wembley, Middx. Telephone: Wembley 3163-6 (4 lines)
Telegrams: Amanco, Phone, London
Scottish Distributors: Cowal Engineering Co., The Ardgoil Works, Tarbet Street, Gourock
Northern Ireland Distributors: The Stanley Motor Works (1932), Ltd., 19a-25, Gt. Victoria St., Belfast

THREE TINS
IN A BOAT

Is there anything more elusive than a farmhouse when you've got milk on your mind? A good reason for packing Nestlé's Milk and lots of it. A better reason is its purity, its richness, its wholesomeness. And the convenience is enormous. No spilling when the boat lurches. No turning sour when the night is sultry. Whatever else you forget, remember Nestlé's Milk for your comfort.

Then there's Ideal — you'll think it's cream but it isn't. It's pure milk concentrated till it is so like cream you can't tell one from the other. Taste it on tinned peaches or fruit salad and know one of the joys of the not-so-simple life.

And then coffee. When you wake and find the morning a little chill— a great steaming, aromatic, bracing mug of Café au Lait. It just means boiling water and two teaspoonfuls out of a tin. As easy as that! Nestlé's Café au Lait is only the finest coffee, the best sugar, the richest milk of dairy cows. No preservative is used and the contents of an opened tin last any reasonable time.

NESTLÉ'S
MILK

IDEAL MILK ❖ CAFÉ AU LAIT

From Grocers Anywhere

SUPERSEDES

METHYLATED

No. 80. Travellers Cooker. 7/6

"META"
THE SAFE SOLID FUEL

Obtainable in Packets   20 Bars. 9d.
"   "   "   50   "   1/9
"   "   "   100   "   2/9

THE FUEL
For Holidays, Motoring,
Camping, Boating, Travelling

ELMEESAN (LONDON) LTD.
86, VICTORIA ST. S.W.1 [WHOLESALE ONLY]

14. Nestlé's in the interwar years. This advertisement was written with the boating holiday in mind.

15. META, the safe solid fuel. In the 1920s it was an indispensable aid to boating holidays.

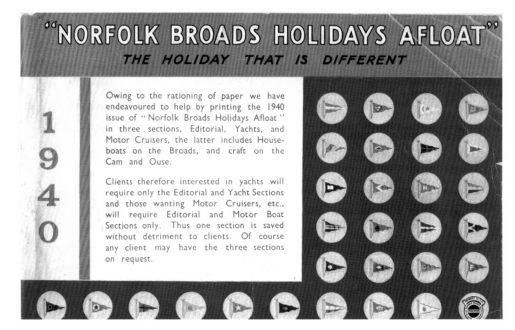

"NORFOLK BROADS HOLIDAYS AFLOAT"
THE HOLIDAY THAT IS DIFFERENT

1940

Owing to the rationing of paper we have endeavoured to help by printing the 1940 issue of "Norfolk Broads Holidays Afloat" in three sections, Editorial, Yachts, and Motor Cruisers, the latter includes House-boats on the Broads, and craft on the Cam and Ouse.

Clients therefore interested in yachts will require only the Editorial and Yacht Sections and those wanting Motor Cruisers, etc., will require Editorial and Motor Boat Sections only. Thus one section is saved without detriment to clients. Of course any client may have the three sections on request.

16. The brochure that never was, Blakes 1940. Owing to the rationing of paper, the company tried to help by printing the brochure in three sections: Editorial, Yachts and Motor Cruisers. The Motor Cruiser section contained the houseboats on the Broads and the 'craft on the Cam and Ouse'. The idea was that clients interested in yachts would need only the yachts and editorial sections. Likewise for those wanting a motor cruiser. There was an optimistic caveat; 'Of course any client may have the three sections on request.'

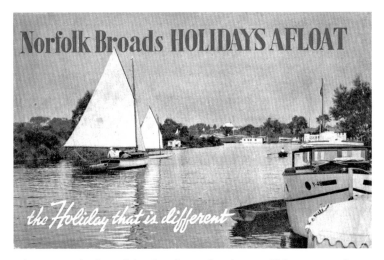

Norfolk Broads HOLIDAYS AFLOAT

the Holiday that is different

Above: 17. The first Blakes brochure after the war. This 1946 catalogue took pains to point out that the official name of the company had changed to BLAKES (Norfolk Broads Holidays) Limited. It went on to explain that they had a new address in Fleet Street, and that Mr and Mrs Blake had now retired. 'The senior staff,' it said, 'remained largely unchanged.' Some of this news, particularly the name change, had been mentioned in the 1940 brochure, but the company was presumably aware of not only having more to say in 1946, but that the 1940 edition had not reached many customers. In an apologetic tone the introduction page of the brochure stated that it was 'not as descriptive' as the company would have liked, but paper rationing still made things difficult. In a more positive note, Blakes stated that they were still the central booking office for all members of the Norfolk and Suffolk Broads Yacht Owners' Association, which had been extended to include 'practically all the Broads boat owners'. The choice of craft was therefore now 'wider than ever before because, more owners than ever before have placed their booking arrangements in our care'.

Below: 18. Advertising in the 1946 Blakes brochure. National brand Heinz also make apologies for the post-war shortages.

Here's hoping . . .

We used to like to think that we added to your enjoyment of holidays afloat by suggesting special stocks of Heinz varieties for the galley.

For flavour is everything in meeting outdoor appetites and the natural flavours of Heinz 57 varieties — so carefully preserved in the cooking — have made them famous.

This year there is little that we dare suggest, though the gradually lifting restrictions on our production may result in a freer choice by the time you take your holiday. For news of that you will have to watch our advertisements in the daily Press.

At the moment you can get Baked Beans, some of the Soups, Spaghetti, Sandwich Spread, and Salad Cream — all of them rich in flavour and nourishment as you know of old.

HEINZ 57 VARIETIES

Always ready to serve

☛ *When in Potter Heigham or Horning, shop at Roys*

PROVISIONS FOR YACHTS

WINES SPIRITS & BEER
MINERAL WATERS

IRONMONGERY, FURNITURE

ROYS
GROCERY & PROVISION STORES

DRAPERY, MILLINERY,
STATIONERY.

TAILORING, OUTFITTING,
FOOTWEAR.

THE WORLD'S LARGEST VILLAGE STORE

THE NORFOLK BROADS SHOPPING CENTRE

ROYS of WROXHAM

GROCERY, PROVISIONS, WINES & SPIRITS, BEER, CIDER, MINERAL WATERS, GREEN FRUITS,
VEGETABLES, FISH, BREAD, MILK, TOBACCO, FISHING TACKLE. METHYLATED
SPIRITS, etc. WIRELESS SETS, GRAMOPHONES & RECORDS for HIRE.
PHARMACY, PHOTOGRAPHIC & CINE SUPPLIES, DEVELOPING & PRINTING.

★ If you don't know what to take, write us; we will | 300 page | We take back any **non-perishable** Goods left over at end of Cruise and
then send you a List of Goods suitable for the Trip. | Price List | allow in full. Goods delivered within 10 miles radius of Wroxham by
| post free | our own vans, or by the most convenient carriers if outside this area.
TO ENSURE EARLY DELIVERY PLEASE SEND YOUR ORDERS IN ADVANCE with Name and Address in Block Capitals.
Branches: HORNING, POTTER HEIGHAM and COLTISHALL.   Telegrams: Roys.   Telephone: 100 (6 lines).

19. Still in 1946 and Roys of Wroxham appear well stocked despite rationing. This is a demonstration of how diverse the company had become by the 1940s and the advertisement contains two key phrases from Roys: the 'World's Largest Village Store' and 'The Norfolk Broads Shopping Centre'.

20. Anchors Aweigh! The 1948 and 1950 editions of the famous Blakes publication. Full of practical hints and information, the 1948 booklet also contained a message from the Broads Protection Society. The society said that every year more and more people visited Broadland to discover what a 'restful, healthy, interesting, instructive and enjoyable holiday' could be obtained there. However, it cautioned, 'steadily nature is causing this once wide three-pronged estuary to diminish and the numbers and sizes of Broads are slowly shrinking'.

Above: 21. October 1949. The wherry *Albion*, restored and on her maiden voyage, is pictured here at Foundry Bridge, Norwich, on her way in from Great Yarmouth. Refurbished and renamed, as she had sailed as *Plane* for many years, Albion has gone on to be a symbol of the Broads.

Within a year of this photograph being taken she'd covered over 2,000 miles, and carried cargo. (Picture by George Plunkett)

Right: 22. Happy Holidaymakers. The Broads 1953. (Picture courtesy of Hoseasons)

23. Refuelling on the Broads in 1953. (Picture courtesy of Hoseasons)

24. The 1952 Hoseason brochure; the 'Bluebird' logo has yet to appear. (Picture courtesy of Hoseasons)

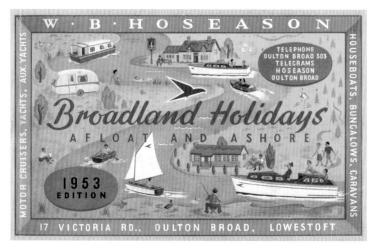

25. The 1953 Hoseasons brochure. It's still W. B. Hoseason, but the new logo has arrived. Graphics are still in use rather than photographs for the front cover. (Picture courtesy of Hoseasons)

26. A 1950s example of integrated marketing. There is everything you need at Wallers Yachting Stores, but remember to say that you booked with Hoseason.

27. Holiday memories. The Broads have been photographed, by professionals and amateurs alike, since cameras were invented. Home movies inevitably followed, as holidaymakers preserved their trips to remember and share with friends and family. This delightful graphic comes from a 1950s Hoseasons publication, and demonstrates cutting-edge technology. By 2013, Broads Tours had introduced a webcam allowing people to log on and see live action from the Broads at any time. Now you could cruise the Broads from your sofa; the Norfolk Broads have never been strangers to innovation. (Picture courtesy of Hoseasons)

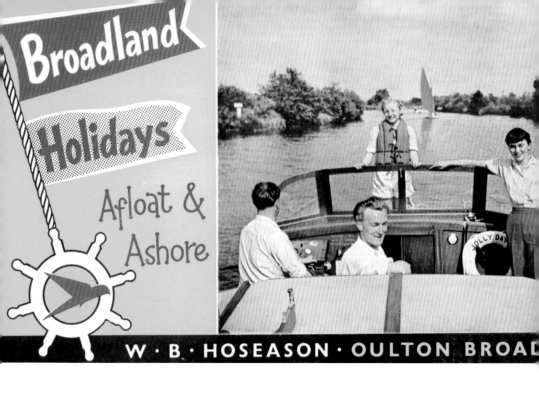

Cruisers Yachts Houseboats Bungalows and Caravans for Holiday Hire

W. B. HOSEASON

89 Bridge Road OULTON BROAD Lowestoft

TEL: OULTON BROAD 136   'GRAMS: HOSEASON, OULTON BROAD

Sole Booking Agent

Dear Reader,
    Have you ever had a holiday where you do exactly as you please all day, every day? A Broadland holiday means complete ~~Freedom~~ glance through the pages that follow and you will

At the time of going to press it has been announced that petrol and other fuel oils will be rationed during 1957. We are, however, assured an ample allocation supply will be available for our hirer's requirements, and cruising will continue.

host of yachts,
om which to choose.
. Our fully
ur service, and
to prove that
cious days.
you in Broadland,

James Hoseason

This page: 28. & 29. It's 1957 and the Hoseason Brochure is embracing holidays afloat and ashore. It has modern graphics and the motor cruiser is in the foreground ... but there were warnings about fuel rationing. (Pictures courtesy of Hoseasons)

SOUTH WALSHAM BROAD, NORFOLK BROADS   15451

This page: 30., 31. & 32. 1960s postcards from the Broads. Who knows how many millions of postcards have been sent on holidays? Although it is almost certainly declining in the Internet age, the postcard was an essential part of a holiday, and Broads holidays were no exception.

THE STARS VISIT BROADLAND

The Broads offer the finest of away-from-it-all hideaways. None know this better than the stars of Cinema and Television. They love to escape from the wear-and-tear of public life to the peace and beauty of Broadland. Here are just some of the celebrities who have found in a Norfolk Holiday the same perfect tranquillity that you will find!

★ **HANK MARVIN**
The Shadows leader says, "Fabulous!" The Young Ones say the Broads are tops. Hank Marvin, leader of the famous Shadows Group, of course chose Hoseasons when he came to book a Norfolk Broads Holiday.

★ **RUSS CONWAY**
Show business can be very exhausting. Through Hoseasons Russ Conway booked a holiday afloat—away from the glare of spotlights and the demand of public life. He found much-needed seclusion on the peaceful Broadland waterways.

★ **KENNETH HORNE**
Mr. Horne says, "I can thoroughly recommend the Norfolk Broads for your next Holiday."

The choice of the famous can easily be yours. No matter what your occupation a holiday at least once a year is needed. There can be no better way of relaxing than enjoying a holiday on the Norfolk Broads.

33. The 1960s, and the stars come out to play on the Norfolk Broads. (Picture courtesy of Hoseasons)

Above left: 34. Happy holidaymakers, 1969-style.

Above right: 35. The family holiday on the Broads in 1969; presumably Dad took the photograph. There's a worrying lack of life jackets by modern standards. (Picture courtesy of Hoseasons)

Above left: 36. The Hoseasons brochure for 1970. Understated personality endorsement and full-colour photography.

Above right: 37. St Benet's Abbey, an integral part of Broads history – and still haunted! (Picture courtesy of Broads Authority)

38. A wherry and a mill: the definitive Broads scene. (Picture courtesy of Broads Authority)

Norfolk Broad...

Holidays Afloat

1956

BLAKES

39. Blakes 1956. The brochure's front cover. 'Dad' is definitely seen as the 'skipper'!

natural beauty; by reason of their holiday and recreational value and the interest of their plant and animal life'.

It was the MP for Lowestoft who would next bring this relationship of holidays and conservation to the fore. As the National Parks debate rumbled on, and against a backdrop of not only the national political scene but considerable confusion and disagreement at local level, he cited the main issues facing the Broads as being silting, pollution and unlawful enclosure. It was, he said in parliament, nothing short of 'sheer robbery' that the local authorities took 'some £6 million' a year in tourist expenditure but did nothing for the upkeep of the Broads as a recreational area. In a to and fro of argument with the Minister for Town and Country Planning, he was told that the Broads were in fact 'on the list' for National Park status, but that the local authorities needed to play their part too. However, despite the Broads being 'on the list', there was the customary caveat that Norfolk was 'different'. The problems were rooted in complications over which local authority was responsible for what. Harbour authorities had control where rivers were tidal, for example. Pollution was someone else's concern. There were, it was said, 'at least a dozen other bodies concerned with the various features of the life of the place'.

The truth is that the question of the Norfolk Broads, and their future as a National Park, was fizzling out. Norfolk was indeed different, and nobody seemed to know how to manage it. Back on the agenda by the early 1960s, the matter still remained unresolved, but the reasons were by now familiar. A 1961 judgement once again stated that the Broads were in no way similar to the other areas that met the criteria for becoming a National Park.

All of this had been going on for years by then, and the great discussions and reports provide a political backdrop for what was happening front of stage. Because if Norfolk's being different was causing the committees consternation, the same quality of being unlike anywhere else was drawing in the holidaymakers.

The Norfolk Broads in the 1950s were experiencing the heyday of the wooden motor cruiser. Initially seen as modern intruders, but soon loved by visitors, the boats are now seen as graceful old-timers themselves, eclipsed by new designs and materials.

It was the world of increased motor car ownership, paid holiday time off work and a chance to enjoy it. The British had not quite yet discovered the European holiday, and a Broads trip was different to the still-popular seaside resort.

The happy family on the cover of the 1956 Blakes brochure, dad with his sailor's cap and cravat, look almost American with their gleaming smiles and jaunty waves. 'Away from bother and business and fuss; away from housework, the job and your old landlocked self – away from it all, to fun and sun, fresh air and freedom,' said the opening page of the giant-size publication.

It's obvious that the 'target audience' was now national. This message was not aimed specifically at Norfolk. In fact, the brochure is almost evangelical in encouraging people to discover and embrace the Broads. 'What a welcome awaits you in Broadland! The warm-hearted and good-humoured local folk have a genuine love for water and boats, and for anyone connected with boats. By taking a holiday afloat you automatically become a patron with a share in the life of this carefree community,' was the decidedly upbeat tone.

Dad was flattered into seeing himself as the skipper, and mum was told that 'cooking is a new pleasure in your craft's neat miniature kitchen'. There was no merging of the gender roles in 1956. But it was of its time, and chatty, inviting and comprehensive in explaining the Broads, the boats and the surrounding area.

As to price, the cost of a holiday varied depending on the boat, of course. If the family on the cover – of mum, dad and one son – were to be catered for, they could, for example, have hired the *Radiant Sun*. This 26-foot motor cruiser from Sun Boats, based at Acle, would cost them £30 for a week in August. The price included insurance, cooking fuel and laundering of the craft's linen. All in, but exclusive of food and other expenses, it sounds cheap by twenty-first-century standards. To put it into context, the average weekly wage for a man over twenty-one at the time was £10 17s 6d.

Anchors Aweigh, the ever helpful handbook, was by 1956 being presented by your 'pilot', Billy Blake. 'Everyone needs a pilot now and then, skipper,' says Billy. And he assured the customer, in his very nautical way, that they'd get their copy of *Anchors Aweigh* before they arrive. 'I'm a-going to send it along to you for sure about a fortnight afore you sets sail,' said Billy, in what was presumably the language of an old Broads sailor.

If Blakes were now directing their message to a national audience, over at Hoseasons the thinking had shifted to address not just who you spoke to, but how and where you spoke to them. They too had realised the importance of a nationwide audience and, unlike some of the political forecasters, saw that the increase in cars meant that people would consider holidays that they'd previously thought inaccessible.

The target had to be the more mobile, and most affluent, consumers. James Hoseason knew how to reach them. Already ramping up his press advertising spaces, he now tested the still-new medium of television. Placing commercials in the London region, he not only reached a cash-rich, holiday-aware audience who would find boating in Norfolk appealing, he also put the brand name into a new market for expansion into holidays on the Thames.

This was a pioneering step. It's important to realise just how new the idea of television advertising was in 1957. It was only two years since Gibbs SR toothpaste had aired the first TV commercial in Britain. Very soon the cigarettes, soap powders and sweets were using television, with a dramatic effect on sales. The petrol brands were there in the early days too, further endorsing that the car was now a central part of family life for the middle classes. But Hoseason was among the first to use TV to promote holidays. Apart from Butlin's, there were few others in 1957.

There were complications for the marketing planners, though. Despite the petrol companies being in the vanguard of television advertising, and the national enthusiasm for motoring, with supreme irony, petrol was in short supply in 1957. The Hoseason brochure for that year carried a message, superimposed on to the page, advising customers that 'at time of going to press' there had been warnings of petrol and fuel oils being rationed in 1957. Under the logo that still said 'W. B. Hoseason' the message, signed by 'James Hoseason', clearly and optimistically stated that 'we are, however, assured an ample allocation supply will be available for our hirer's requirements and cruising will continue'. The facts, spelled out, with the personal touch of the signature. This was a company in tune with its market.

In the world of advertising and marketing, the Norfolk Broads had an interesting and short-lived encounter with footwear in the 1950s. Norwich-based shoe manufacturer Van Dal had decided to concentrate on making wider-fitting shoes for women. Given their East Anglian location, the company called the shoes the 'Norfolk Broads'. Everything was fine until the overseas agents pointed out that a 'Broad' might mean a charming stretch of water in Norfolk, but in other parts of the world it referred to a lady, and not in a nice way. The name was changed.

The Broads had by now a long-established link to the nation's cultural life; painters, artists, writers, and photographers had been drawn to the Broads for centuries. In the 1950s, the cinema was an important part of the average family's entertainment, and Norfolk and the Broads area made it to the big screen. In 1951, filmgoers had been watching *The Case of the Missing Scene*. This crime caper was set in the fictional Norfolk village of Poldyke and told the story of a film crew and some poachers, all of whom, but for different reasons, are on the trail of the bittern. A children's film, made by a briefly separate department of the Rank Organisation, it was the directorial début of Don Chaffey, who went on to direct major science fiction films, including *Jason and the Argonauts* (1963) and *One Million Years BC* (1966).

Of all the celebrities to have direct links to the Broads, the one who characterised the 1950s was George Formby. A huge star since the 1930s, Formby had first visited the Broads in the 1940s. He loved the area and bought a house there. It was called Heronby, and was on the river near Wroxham. In 1953, he bought a boat.

Traumerei was a motor cruiser, built by Windboats in 1950. George renamed her *Lady Beryl* after his wife. Sadly, we now know that George and Beryl's marriage was far from idyllic, but they were show business royalty in the 1950s and appearances counted.

In fact, George commissioned a second boat in 1957, also from Windboats, and he christened her *Lady Beryl II*. It has been suggested that George loved the water so much that the house at Wroxham was barely lived in, he and Beryl, despite the tensions between them, spending their time on the boats. George was often seen calling at riverside shops to buy a paper, using as transport a 14-foot wooden launch built by Herbert Woods.

Not everybody had their own private boat, of course. But post-war life was improving for many and the increasingly popular car was by now having a real impact on the railways. Just as the train had affected the old waterborne transport, so now it became vulnerable to the road. There were concerns, too, over the network in general, and Dr Beeching's axe was not far away. The main lines to get to the county had survived, but the internal connections were dramatically reduced. It was as if the county had become even more mysterious to those who lived in the industrial conurbations or commuter belts.

A lot had happened in what was a short period since the end of the war. Now, just fifteen years after VE Day, a rationing-free, television-watching, NHS-supported public could visit the Norfolk Broads to find modern post-war boats with full facilities on board. Local pubs and hotels offered increasingly well-organised catering and entertainment. The booking process was slick and designed to meet your every need. The issues over conservation, and the National Park politics, were being played out in the committee rooms, but in consumer land the country was gearing up for the 1960s. For a moment, there was little interest in looking back, or holding back. It was time to have a good time.

1960–1970

The problem was that it wasn't all good news for the Norfolk Broads from a commercial point of view. The increasingly affluent consumer had discovered Europe, and the holiday companies had met the demand to get there with the package holiday. Suddenly, there was guaranteed sunshine and there were new things to discover. It's true that many of the first British tourists on package holidays did not always embrace the local food, and this was the era when a straw donkey keepsake could be bought without irony. However, the fact was that the UK holiday industry in general, and the Norfolk Broads was no exception, needed to fight harder for the holiday pound it had been collecting in bigger quantities since 1945.

The Broads business had indeed got bigger. There were now serious worries over congestion on the waterways, as well as real concerns about the erosion being caused by heavier boat traffic. By 1963, more legislation was being discussed and there were proposals for the cutting out of new basins to reduce congestion at popular moorings, as well as for dredging and clearance programmes. The question of a speed limit was also being discussed.

Outside of the holiday season, work was seriously hampered in the winter of 1962/3. Broadland froze in what is now recognised as the coldest winter on record. Snow had fallen on Boxing Day 1962, following what had been a bad period of weather prior to Christmas.

From that point on the temperatures plummeted and the snow lay around until March. Broads and rivers froze. Skating and walking were common on the ice. By modern, or any, standards, some activities were dangerous. There are several accounts of people driving cars on the frozen surfaces of rivers and Broads. The conditions affected every aspect of agriculture, transport and domestic life. The effect on wildlife was palpable. There is little doubt that the dreadful winter of 1963 contributed to the final demise of the controversial coypu.

The coypu is an odd and recurring part of the Norfolk Broads story. This South American water rodent was taken to Europe, and North America, to be farmed for its fur. In the 1920s and 1930s, coypu were brought to Norfolk where they were established in farms. Keeping them in the farms was the problem – coypu escaped. They bred at an alarming rate and estimates put the adult population at one point as around 5,000.

Control programmes, and eventually the legendary winter of 1963, were credited with wiping them out. The coypu is tenacious, however, and occasional sightings are claimed to this day.

While they were numerous the coypu were the cause of serious damage. They gnawed their way through vegetation and were generally considered to be the culprits for the loss of reed beds and accelerating erosion of the banks. Later investigation showed that, in the case of the banks, both man and nature had contributed to the erosion. Neither was the sole cause, but the coypu and the new motor cruisers had to share the blame.

Commercially, the Broads were undergoing more change. While Hoseasons and Blakes still dominated the market, another business was coming alongside. The Caister Group, who owned holiday camps as well as a hundred or so Broads boats, began to flex its muscles. During 1965 they increased their portfolio significantly. They acquired a boatyard and fleet from Herbert Freeman in Beccles. But then, dramatically, they bought not just the Southgates fleet in Horning but also the renowned Herbert Woods operation at Potter Heigham. Next came the Easticks yard, with its twenty-plus boats, at Acle. By the time they had absorbed Norfolk Holiday Boats, the Caister Group had built up a fleet of over 330 boats. Suddenly, and quietly, they'd become the biggest fleet under single control on the Broads.

The Blakes and Hoseasons fleets were seemingly bigger, but the fact was that neither of the companies owned any of the boats they marketed. Blakes, which had started as an agency, was now a co-operative of owners. It was an association, and a capital 'A' for association was, confusingly for some, the logo for Blakes.

Hoseason, whose flag was by now the ubiquitous 'Bluebird' logo, was not an owner either. In almost a reversal of roles the newer company had grown from boatyard to letting agency, whilst the older organisation had shifted from lettings agency to 'association of owners'.

Other owners and yards were operating too, but the increasingly effective marketing of the big players was having a real effect. Successful in gaining business in the face of the European package holiday, it was creating so much traffic on the Broads that the dilemma now was very much what had been suggested in the 1950 edition of *Anchors Aweigh*. Leaving aside conservation in the purest sense, there was a need to dredge, clean and open up any restricted waterways so that the holiday industry had room to manoeuvre. It was either that, or reduce and regulate the number of boats on the Broads.

It was a pressing issue. Despite changes in volume of trade, the freight-carrying boats, on the Yare in particular, were getting bigger. It was a two-way street; the size of these boats were posing a danger to sailors, let alone holiday craft crewed by amateurs. But, despite advice from the likes of 'Pilot Billy Blake', the holidaymakers were ignoring signs and mooring on bends. Accidents and collisions became increasingly common.

One man's congestion is another's bustling activity. The problems that needed addressing were of course the direct result of thousands of people enjoying themselves. The rivers and Broads were crowded, but that meant you were holidaying in a popular 'place to be seen'. After all, Cliff Richard was on holiday there in the summer of 1965! This was no longer somewhere associated with the much loved pre-war stars now falling from fashion like George Formby. This was a modern holiday destination. The fact that it was 'bustling' meant you got to meet other holidaymakers. If you ran a business in Norfolk it meant you met lots of customers. Somehow this had to be continually developed, because it was now a vital part of the local economy. And somehow it had to retain the charm of the area, while meeting increasingly high customer expectations for the modern holiday.

Plainly, the boats themselves were an obvious opportunity for modernisation. With the demise of the commercial wherry, and the arrival of the motor cruiser still within living memory, the next innovation arrived. It was almost inevitable that it would be the 1960s that saw the introduction of the fibreglass boat.

As with so many late twentieth-century innovations, the earliest work done on plastics and new materials for boatbuilding was a direct result of the war. Further experiments during the early 1950s meant that by the 1960s there was a new alternative. Aside from commercial and naval shipping, boats had been made from wood since ancient history. Now there was the fibreglass hull.

Fibreglass, or GRP, for glass reinforced plastic, is a strong but lightweight material. It can be shaped and moulded, and it was ideal for building a new type of boat. Broom Boats were among the first of the Broadland yards to make a start working with GRP. It was Martin Broom who set up a company to make fibreglass hulls, and Aquafibre would ultimately become part of the Broom company.

Some of the earliest boats had GRP hulls coupled with traditional wooden superstructures, but by the end of the 1960s the completely fibreglass boat was very much the standard.

There was, and in some quarters still is, some negative reaction to the new boats. But then the wooden motor cruiser had once been seen as a modern intruder, and the stark reality is that the vast majority of Broads holidaymakers were not boating traditionalists. They *needed* craft that were easy to maintain, difficult to damage, easy to repair and simple to navigate. They *wanted* craft that were spacious, modern, comfortable and in keeping with the 1960s and not-so-distant 1970s. The truth was that the fibreglass boat delivered all of that.

The Caribbean cruiser was first seen at the 1965 Boat Show. Introduced by F. B. Wilds, it caused a storm among boating purists. Some called it a 'plastic bath tub'.

In 1951, Frank Wilds, a building contractor, had been watching a boat race on Barton Broad, where Nelson had learned to sail in the previous century. He'd been smitten with boating from that moment and, using his builder's skills, constructed his own boat from plans in the *Motor Boat and Yachting Manual* he bought at W H Smith. He put the finished 17-foot boat on a lorry, brought it to Norfolk, entered the next year's race, and won.

He moved to Horning in 1953, with plans for at least partial retirement, but things worked out differently. Having built a house and bought a cruiser, he was settling in to a different lifestyle when he heard of someone who wanted a boat on which to cruise the Broads. It seemed that they owned a boat but it couldn't negotiate the bridge at Great Yarmouth. There was a suggestion that Frank let them rent his cruiser. The idea for this short-term, one-off hiring came from none other than James Hoseason. It proved to be a catalyst. By 1964, Frank Wild was in the boat-hire business proper.

Ever enterprising, he decided to use a boat of his own design. It was the Caribbean. Unconventional and modern, with a cockpit arrangement that brought criticism from some quarters, it proved safe and ideal for the amateur. Soon the pale-blue Caribbean cruisers would be a familiar sight on the Norfolk Broads. It was often more appreciated by those on board than by those observing from the shore.

The next few years would see other new classes of boat arrive in the hire fleets. From Porter and Haylett in Wroxham came the fibreglass Catalina 35, which was in the Hoseason fleet by 1972. At the same time, five of the new Dancing Light class from Aquafibre were being let by Blakes for the Herbert Woods yard in Potter Heigham. Again, the class was fibreglass in construction, and the launch details proudly explained that the boats not only had showers, two toilets, razor points and melamine surfaces, but a cocktail cabinet too.

Modernising the Broads holiday industry took more than changing the construction methods of the boats, though. The marketing and advertising strategies were increasingly sophisticated. Certainly the use of coupons you clipped out to order your new brochure had now developed to the point where code numbers indicated precisely which publications produced the greatest response. This data were then used to plan the next burst of activity, constantly refining the allocation of the advertising budget to ensure maximum results and high cost-efficiency.

Both the main companies were using a wider and wider spread of media, determined to win business from as many consumers as possible. Over and above the main national press, campaigns appeared in the angling magazines, the birdwatching publications and the yachting press, because there were keen sailors who couldn't afford a boat of their own.

By the mid-1960s, television was firmly established compared to those fledgling days of 1957. This was the era of the big TV stars and massive audiences for the small number of terrestrial channels. It's of less importance in the twenty-first century, because of the internet and digital programme guides, but in the 1960s the 'Christmas Double Issues' of the *Radio Times* for BBC programmes, and the *TV Times* for the ITV schedules, were an essential family purchase. This was where you found out which films were on which day, and the times of the big Christmas specials featuring the stars. Video recording had not arrived, so planning your viewing was an essential part of Christmas.

Assiduously studied to plan seasonal viewing, these bumper magazines had another vital purpose. Research of spending patterns had shown that, although taken in the summer, most UK holidays were booked in the winter. It wasn't difficult to work out. People decided on the holiday and then needed time to put money aside for it. A deposit at time of booking would reserve it, but six months or so to get the rest of the price together was essential.

This, together with holiday companies needing to plan their own business years, meant that Christmas was the peak booking period. There are often comments now on how Christmas arrives in the shops before summer is over, or how early the first Easter egg can be spotted after New Year. It's all part of the ever accelerating seasons. In Britain in the early to mid-1960s, these patterns were less frenetic. But Boxing Day was established as a key tipping point in holiday bookings and more people watched TV at Christmas than at any other time. The strategy then was to advertise on television over Christmas, and tell people that your advertisement was in the press. Especially the TV magazines. That was essential because the newspaper coupon was still the best way for the customer to interact with the company. How else would they get their brochure? Interactive websites were unimaginable, even in the swinging, technological sixties.

The brochure was essential to selling holidays. It was the 'shop window'. Armed with a brochure full of boats and, increasingly, shore properties, the consumer made their choice and booked their holiday. As innovative as the Broads holiday companies were, the basis of the 'selling chain' had remained unaltered for decades. The boats were being modernised; now it was time to do more.

All of the organisations actively marketing holidays on the Norfolk Broads at this point saw the need, and responded. Those that didn't would not survive. It must be said that it was perhaps Jimmy Hoseason who embraced the marketing concept more readily than most. A driven man, he had both natural business acumen and a scientific approach to promotion. Perhaps more important than anything, he saw the business as a whole.

That meant starting inside. Training was vital to the Hoseason ethic. Famously intolerant of mediocrity, James Hoseason and his team ensured that every member of staff was trained to do their job, whatever that role within the company was, to the highest standard possible. And all standards and objectives were directed towards one common goal: customer satisfaction.

Attention to detail was another ruthlessly pursued philosophy. This wasn't a 'look after the pennies and the pounds will look after themselves' attitude, rooted in a belief that if you get the little things right the big things will just happen. The big picture, or overall strategy, was clearly in place and honed to perfection. It was a zealous belief that the strategy was worthless unless every tiny detail involved in its implementation was polished and perfectly placed. It's what made the machine work.

The next objective was to make it work faster. Hoseasons broke the bonds of the traditional selling chain. Installing answering machines on phone lines and advertising 'Dial-A-Brochure' as a service was tantamount to switching on the turbocharger. Consumers could see the advertisement in the Saturday and Sunday papers, as they had for some years. There were the Christmas TV magazines, and all the other specific sectors too. But now, instead of at worst never getting round to it, and at best getting the coupon in Monday morning's post, somebody could make a phone call right away, twenty-four hours a day. All they had to do was leave their name and address on the answering service, and the brochure was dispatched the next day at the latest. Not only did it speed up the process for both the customer and the company, it also felt right. It was modern. It was marketing so good that you didn't feel you were being sold to; you felt you were being looked after. And you were.

By the time there was an added service that let you actually book your holiday by phone, and, for maximum convenience, let you do it on a Sunday evening, the strategy was near perfect.

But still the pursuit of the ideal service continued. Not entirely alone, but certainly unusually for a company of their size and type, Hoseasons engaged in further research that proved two things. Firstly, people still decided on where they were going to go for a holiday first, and then what activity or type of holiday they would have there. The purely boating element of Hoseasons advertising became secondary to the location. It was a tactic applied throughout the increasingly national operation, but it certainly applied to advertising for boats on the Norfolk Broads. It could be argued that this was an endorsement of some of the strategies employed by others decades earlier, implemented without the benefit of research. The point was that it had been tested, and that planning was now more informed.

Next, when it came to who booked the holiday, there was no doubt. The man paid, but the woman chose. She also set the budget. And, as it was a self-catering holiday, the woman needed to feel that she was having a break too. The Hoseasons campaigns started to acknowledge all of that, but beyond the advertising the product itself was developed to match the market. Now, there were more kitchen gadgets, and fridge space was made available. There were duvets and storage space. Marketing is about meeting customers' needs, and Hoseasons were setting a new standard in doing just that.

1970–1980

By the 1970s the Norfolk Broads were, in their perennial dual identity, a world-class holiday destination, ably and professionally marketed by local companies, as well as an internationally renowned area of natural beauty and importance. The landscape of the area was instantly recognisable. The wide Norfolk skies, the low horizon pierced by sails and masts. A million images of the Norfolk Broads were, even in a pre-Internet world, reproduced for all to see. Postcards, pamphlets and souvenirs were bought and given, fuelling ever greater awareness of this piece of England that, like Norfolk in general, was loved by those who had come to know it and often misunderstood by those who hadn't.

Even that other symbol of the Broads skyline, the windmill, was often assumed to be a sign that Norfolk had a proliferation of traditional mills to grind corn. Many a visitor, and student, has had to have explained to them that the vast majority of these 'mills' were in fact wind pumps.

Windmills and Wind Pumps

A flat horizon, a sail, a big sky and a windmill are almost essential ingredients in any picture that wants to say 'Norfolk Broads'. Painters and photographers have always used the mill as a subject in Norfolk views. Some Norfolk mills were used to grind corn but the vast majority were built to help in the constant battle to manage the landscape and drain the ditches and dykes.

A Norfolk wind pump almost grew out of the landscape. The workers, with all the materials, would have got to the site by river to start building. Working on the riverbank, with the vast timbers, they would have constructed the 'mill' and its adjacent cottage.

Once installed, the millwright, who was often a marsh man, would begin a life of hard and lonely work. He was often responsible for keeping several miles of river clear and at the right level. The fear was flooding, and it was an endless winter vigil beneath the swirling sails to maintain the drainage. Even so, in better weather, the millwrights often took extra, often quite menial, agricultural jobs to survive.

The last wind pump to be built on the Broads is now one of the best-known. Fully operational until 1943, when it was struck by lightning, Horsey Mill was bought by the National Trust in 1948. The owners had been the Buxton family, and they continue to manage the lands around the now restored mill. A classic Norfolk mill, it attracts enormous numbers of visitors, who also enjoy the walks through what is an internationally famous wildlife area. Horsey Mill itself is a Grade II listed building.

Many of the wind pumps, like Horsey, worked for decades, even seeing off competition from steam- and eventually diesel-powered pumps. The flat landscape and the great sails were an ideal combination, catching the stiff winds that cut across the marshes. Ultimately it was electricity that proved their downfall.

Many still stand, some of them having been restored. In total there are over seventy, in various states of repair, visible in Norfolk. A singular claim to fame goes to Sutton Mill. This eighteenth-century structure, with nine floors, is the country's tallest surviving windmill.

Arguably primitive in their engineering, but wholly effective in their work, these great towers of energy no longer hold back the waters, but they still, instantly, say Norfolk.

Just as it had in the eighteenth and nineteenth centuries, Norfolk, and the Broads, appeared in both high art and popular culture. Ransome's books were, as ever, still in print, weathering the changes in fashion and style. Rather more 'modern' young Broads adventurers had appeared in novels such as *A Camp under Sail* by Stanley Holbrooke-Jones.

Crime had reared its head, in a fictional sense. The prolific and important crime writer Gladys Mitchell featured St Helens church at Ranworth in her novel *Wraiths and Changelings*. It was Mitchell who, among a vast output, also wrote *The Nodding Canaries*. The town of 'Nodding' is plainly a thinly disguised Norwich.

Another curious shift from the real location of Norfolk occurs in the crime writing of Alan Hunter. The immensely popular George Gently books were written by this Norfolk man, and set in Norfolk. Oddly, when they were understandably deemed ideal for televising, the action and characters were relocated to the North East.

The poet George Macbeth had moved to Norfolk in the late 1970s and it was from Oby, near the River Bure, that he wrote and set some of his work.

And if there were ever a reference in popular culture that spoke volumes about the polarising world of holidays, it was certainly David Bowie's. While not actually a lyric about vacations, his 1971 song 'Life on Mars' put into the English language the phrase 'From Ibiza to the Norfolk Broads'.

The Broads had continued their links with show business stars. Many of them were in the area as they played summer seasons at the coastal resorts. Others had simply seen the attraction of the area, and perceived its quieter waterways as a means of escaping their busy schedules. Cliff Richard, and George Formby before him, had been visible on the Broads, but the late 1960s and certainly the 1970s saw a more positive embracing of celebrity.

The Hoseason brochure for 1970 is very aware of star potential. The Norfolk Broads, we're told, are 'a favourite haunt of the stars of the entertainment world. Eve Boswell, Russ Conway, Dick Emery, and Pat Phoenix'.

Phoenix was by then a household name owing to her Coronation Street character Elsie Tanner. Her having holidayed with Hoseason in 1969 and rebooking in 1970 certainly warranted the colour picture of her at the wheel of a boat. It didn't matter if people identified her as Pat Phoenix or the controversial but much-loved Elsie. This was almost as valuable as TV advertising itself. It was an A-grade television-star endorsement.

By now the company was using the national network of TV stations to promote their complete portfolio of holidays, with the Norfolk Broads as a key element. The reworking of 'Messing about on the River' as the soundtrack became virtually a signature tune.

As Hoseasons continually modernised and marketed, their long-time competitor, Blakes, was also making big changes in the early 1970s. After over sixty years, they officially moved back to Norfolk. Despite their reorganisation into more of a Broads co-operative, they had always operated from a London office. From the original premises set up by Harry Blake in Basinghall Street, they'd moved to Newgate Street during the First World War, and on to Fleet Street by 1945. From there they'd set up base in Piccadilly. Now they 'came home' to where Harry Blake, all those years ago, had hired a boat from Ernest Collins and, at the end of his holiday, had suggested he become an agent for them, certain that he could get more bookings, and extend the season, by being more organised.

Organisation was very much the message that Blakes spread as part of the announcement concerning their move to Norfolk. Their 1908 catalogue had listed just over forty yachts for hire across a six-week season. As the 1970s got into swing Blakes were offering some 1,300 craft, and the season spanned twenty weeks.

From the new offices in Wroxham there was to be a new, streamlined booking system, very much geared to the telephone. Colour-coded charts would allow the 'booking clerk' to establish availability of precisely the type of boat best suited to the customer. Blakes (Norfolk Broads Holidays Afloat) was now available on a string of Wroxham phone numbers, each of which was linked to different sizes and capacities of boat.

However, as the Broads holiday industry was powering ahead, there were moves to slow things down. There had been a decision, or at least a proposal, to impose speed restrictions on boats. In 1971, the Yare Commissioners took action. They imposed a 5 mph limit on boats travelling between Norwich and the New Cut. This was aimed at slowing down traffic in the built-up areas where small boats were often moored.

Suggestions for some 7 mph limits had fallen by the wayside, but the new 5 mph restriction meant that there were now only some 12 miles of the river free of limits. The 5 mph limit would apply to the river from Trowse almost to Postwick. Surlingham Broad, Rockland Broad, the Chet and the Wensum from New Mills in Norwich to where it joined the Yare were all now controlled.

Reaction to the speed limit question came from several quarters. Brooms the boatbuilder took issue as they claimed it prevented them from testing new craft. A rather more unexpected protest came from the waterskiing fraternity, who pointed out that it rendered their sport almost impossible. There was much cut and thrust in the arguments, and press coverage was balanced in that it reported all sides.

As the test-running and waterskiing arguments aired, so too did the conservation point of view, coupled with opinions of local residents. In 1976, a spokesman for the Nature Conservancy Council went so far as to say that he gave the Broads 'another ten years before they reached to the point of no return'.

There was by now a 'squad' of twelve inspectors, using a dozen launches, patrolling the Broads, and they claimed that speeding motor cruisers were their biggest worry.

Their argument was widening. Firstly they were concerned about the banks being washed away, but with that was their anxiety over pollution, fish being killed and wildlife being scared away. There was also a feeling that the river traffic was akin to the then much-publicised issue of road safety. Accidents on the Broads were not, it was admitted, as frequent or 'catastrophic' as incidents on the road, but the 5 mph and 7 mph speed limits were as essential as the 50 mph and 70 mph restrictions on cars. Those breaking the limits on the rivers were referred to, very much in the parlance of the time, as 'speed merchants', and there was to be no hesitation in bringing them to court.

There was talk of deposits being retained by boatyards to settle fines should they be incurred, and spot fines were discussed, although, bringing in the parallel with the roads again, it was thought that these would not see the light of day until they were applied to motorists as well. A press article of 1976 brought the discussion to a balanced close by pointing out that the 'speed merchants' were in the minority, and that most people stuck to the rules.

Control and legislation was under discussion constantly, but some developments during the mid-1970s show how complex the picture was, and is.

Hoseasons and Blakes had joined forces in 1974 to issue a statement or 'memorandum' concerning the issue of pollution. The problem was that they wanted to ensure that the 150-or-so sailing boats on the Broads would remain exempt from the conditions of the Protection of the Environment Bill. Local by-laws exempted the Norfolk Broads sailing yachts from the rules regarding the discharging of polluting matter. The more modern, and larger, boats had by now been fitted with waste containment systems. The two companies pointed out that it simply wasn't practical to install such a system on the older, and smaller, cabin sailing yachts.

In detail, they said that, apart from the fact that a partly full tank would probably spill during 'tacking', which yachts needed to do, a system on board would mean that the cabin roof would have to be raised in order to use the toilet. This couldn't be done without shifting the beam, which was not possible during sailing. There were only a few boats affected and the hope was that they would be exempt from the proposed legislation.

It's of interest that in the following year, 1975, the redoubtable Ted Ellis made a telling point in the great debate of conservation versus recreation.

In May that year, he had said at a meeting in Norwich that the Broads, 'once a paradise of wildlife', was dying. Speaking in his capacity as vice-chairman of the Norfolk Naturalists Trust, he was commenting on some work carried out by a team from the University of East Anglia. Their findings showed that out of some twenty-eight areas investigated, eleven appeared to be devoid of aquatic vegetation, and a further eleven showed poor growth.

Ellis explained that the trust now owned some 2,300 acres of Broadland and planned to spend up to £250,000, over ten years, to research the decline in wildlife. Referring back to the areas researched by the university, and presumably also commenting on the future, he said that that there was 'a multiple pollution problem of boating, excessive agricultural fertilizer draining from the land and effluent from sewage works'.

Importantly in this ongoing debate and at this time of tourism development, he made the point that he 'did not think holidaymakers were primarily to blame'. The balance was being weighed again. This time, however, it wasn't simply recreation and conservation. Industrialisation was in the frame too.

Through all of this discussion and concern over the future of the Broads, in 1976, a survivor of it all sailed back into the foreground. The *Albion*, by then the last trading sailing wherry, began her journey towards restoration.

Now nearly eighty years old, *Albion* had been bought by the Norfolk Wherry Trust in 1949, and the plan was to preserve her as a working, rather than static, reminder of the great Broads boats. She began what had been christened 'Wherry Week' by visiting Surlingham Ferry.

If there was any 'competition' in terms of press coverage and visibility for the various bodies and camps of Broadland, it was another visitor in 1976 who grabbed the headlines for the Norfolk Naturalists Trust. Her Majesty the Queen was in Ranworth to open the new Broadland Conservation Centre. Together with the Duke of Edinburgh, she had flown in to RAF Coltishall and, after a drive to Horning Green Staithe, she appropriately took a river trip to Ranworth.

There she opened and inspected the new centre and nature trail. The purpose of the project was to educate and enthuse people about the natural history of the Broads, and to make conservation a more accessible concept to everybody. The centre was very much aimed at the amateur and visitor as well as the more informed nature watcher. Schoolchildren and local inhabitants were as much the target audience as Broads holidaymakers.

The Norfolk Naturalists Trust had commissioned architects Fielding and Mawson to design and build the centre on land ideally suited to the purpose. It was isolated, had water and land access and offered stunning views of the surrounding countryside. Because it was so visible, the design was deliberately sympathetic to the environment. Built on pontoons, it was protected from flooding as well as being mobile. It could be towed to alter its position and to move it for winter maintenance.

However, if conservation was making the headlines because it was, seemingly, making headway, the opinions expressed at a county council meeting in 1977 painted a blacker picture. There was, though, some indication that something must be done about it.

In a 31–17 vote that split the Conservative majority, Norfolk County Council agreed that a single National Park committee could preserve the future of the Broads. The – admittedly minority – objectors claimed that this would bring in more tourists and add another level of bureaucracy to local government. In a forthright rebuttal, Ian Coutts, then leader of the council Conservative group, said that the truth was 'we have failed'.

The National Park Question – Back on the Table

The National Park question was very much back on the table. 'Multitudinous bodies' had not delivered the level of care needed, it was said. Ian Coutts believed that a single authority had to be the way forward. 'The Broads are polluted. The fish are dying. The Broads are overcrowded. They are full of rubbish on the banks. The things we seek to look after there are really not being terribly well looked after at all,' he said. Stating that he had talked to councillors in other parts of the country who had claimed that a National Park system worked well, he reiterated the notion of failure to date. 'It is because we have failed that we must look to some other form of organisation to achieve the ends we want.'

Against claims that such a committee would have limited powers, he said that their brief could be extended. In a telling realisation of how popular the Broads already were, he pointed out that National Park status would not produce a sudden influx of tourists. The people were coming anyway.

He was supported by the Hon. Robin Walpole as chairman of the Planning and Transportation Committee. In a demonstration of how the Broads can raise passions across all boundaries, he gained further, if perhaps unexpected, support from Leonard Stevenson of the Labour group.

But this was not a 'done deal'. Mr Adrian Gunson argued that the Broads were unsuitable as a National Park, 'without harmony of interest or communications'. There were, he said, faults in development control, and that needed new changes in planning, not a new authority such as a National Park which *would* bring in a new influx of tourists to the already overcrowded Broads.

Commander Mike Cheyne joined the furore by saying that £120,000 had already been spent on the Broads by the Port and Haven Commissioners 'from charges and dues' and with the Water Authority already in place he didn't want the Countryside Commission 'stamping in the area'.

There were feelings from others that the district councils and drainage boards were all perfectly aware of the Broads' problems and that they were the best people to deal with them. Was this an attempt, asked others, for the county to get back its planning powers through a National Park committee?

Earlier in the meeting, Commander Cheyne had made another point. He suggested that any decision be deferred until it could be made in the light of findings from a forthcoming seminar. There was a danger that to decide before then would be dangerously devoid of facts. Quoting Harry Truman, he pointedly said to the Hon. Robin Walpole, 'I have made up my mind, don't confuse me with me the facts.'

This was a highly charged conversation. The seminar to which Commander Cheyne had referred was organised by the School of

Environmental Sciences and the Centre of East Anglian Studies at the University of East Anglia.

'The Future of Broadland', as the seminar, or forum, was entitled, proved to be a more-than-interesting set of views. In many ways the participants, and the discussions they had, encapsulated all of the elements in this story so far. It was a crystallisation of every aspect of the great Broads debate.

The forum was held, it was explained, as the result of 'increasing evidence of severe pollution and its consequences, continuing pressure of use, leading to conflict between different types of user, and a diversity of authorities responsible for the area and its management'.

Straight away, all the recently raised points were covered. The situation had resulted in a recent suggestion by the Countryside Commission that Broadland be designated a National Park and 'perhaps it is the present scale and rapidity of change that makes the public debate on the issue the more urgent'.

Because much of the research work aimed at finding out more about deterioration on the Broads was carried out at the University of East Anglia, the forum was, very largely, organised by Dr Brian Moss, who led the team there.

An 'Introduction to the Ecology of Broadland and its Problems' was the opening stage. The speakers were Dr M. George, the Regional Officer, East Anglian Region, of the Nature Conservancy Council, and Ted Ellis (Dr E. A. Ellis) from the Norfolk Naturalists Trust.

Dr George made some interesting points. He spoke of the changes that had occurred, particularly since 1950, and the reduction in vegetation and wildlife. As his case developed, though, he touched on the work done by Dr Moss and the fact that the findings showed a marked increase of phosphates in the water. This caused several serious problems. Where it all came from was interesting in itself. Sewage works were definitely responsible to a degree. So too were seagulls. A large roost at Hickling was causing phosphates from the natural world.

His overall point was to prove just how complex and interrelated the problems were, and that research was not only proving that, but showing that something had to be done.

If there was to be a comment about modern marketing techniques, the likely target was the holiday industry on the Broads. Instead, the world of consumerism came in for a different line of attack from Ted Ellis. On the question of phosphates he opened by saying that he thought farmers were generally law-abiding folk and that they were aware of, and working on, the problems. His real worry was the effluent from sewage. 'In the old days,' he said, the effluent from Whitlingham sewage works had been 'alright' until washing powders were used. His idea was that the soap powder manufacturers, then famous for their '1p and 2p off' offers, should, instead of taking money off, either hold the price or put money on, and the chemical industries who make the washing powders be approached for money, raised in this way, to help the cause.

In a more nostalgic bent, and referring to the National Park question, Ellis referred to the work of Lord Somerleyton, saying that the work he had done at Fritton Lake had in effect created a sort of 'National Park' there already. He mused on it being as nice as the days when his mother was 'a child 100 years ago, when they used to have strawberry picnics there and go boating'.

This sudden flashback to an earlier stage of the Broads history was more than simply romantic. It opened up a point he would drive home, and one that would be amplified in the same forum. Fritton Lake, he said, 'had not been spoiled by the encouragement of people to go there and enjoy themselves'. He did qualify that by saying to enjoy themselves 'in a gentle way'.

Ellis had been speaking as a council member of the Norfolk Naturalists Trust. It's not to say that he was expressing a view with which they did not agree, but the trust did put forward their 'official' or 'corporate' stance.

They had decided to 'make up their own mind' on the documents they had received from the Countryside Commission. They were significant landowners in Broadland, and a charitable organisation.

In expressing their view they raised a point which constantly lurks in the background of the Broads and their conservation. By now, of course, it was known that this unique wetland area of outstanding beauty was in fact largely man-made anyway. This had obviously been pointed out in the to and fro of argument and the trust had an answer. It was true, they said, that people had dug holes in a marshy landscape for peat. But they had done it in an area where natural rivers ran through them and the wildlife had simply made use of the results after man had abandoned them.

Now, it was different. Man was interfering 'very considerably'. Their case then took some unexpected twists and turns. Not surprisingly, they admitted that pollution was a worry. They acknowledged that 'people had said there were too many boats', but this was instantly qualified by saying that the boat operators had shown much goodwill, and that practical measures, such as the waste containment systems, had been brought in. The River Authority had been instrumental in this. But, in a charming reference to the oft quoted Norfolk attitude of doing things differently or doing their 'own thing' the trust then went on to say that 'we do not want people from national government interfering with us'. 'You only want to go to them when you want a lot of money' was the arguably contentious view.

The trust did go on to explain that they felt there was a need for a cohesive effort in managing the Broads, and that they had looked carefully at the National Parks concept. Acknowledging that farmers had issues over footpaths and access, and that all the other problems needed addressing, their view was that the National Park idea as it existed probably would not work for the Broads. However, echoing a sentiment from the earlier council meeting, if such an authority had extended powers, then it could be the answer.

The final part of their expression of views was abundantly clear. The Anglian Water Authority needed to pull its weight because they had an enormous stake in the Broads, and could do a lot towards cleaning up the water. When it came to people visiting the area, and the number of boats, it was the trust who owned most of the Broads and surrounding land, so they were deeply involved with, and concerned about, the need to protect the environment and the heritage.

> We want you to enjoy it, we want the people from away, as well as Norfolk people, to enjoy this country as far as it is possible to do so without destroying it. That, in a nutshell, is our attitude. We are inclined to listen to the National Parks suggestion and to support them in exploring this further.

In making his submission to this plainly informative and thought-provoking forum, Martin Shaw, then County Planning Officer, provided some useful statistics that confirmed the position of Broadland at the time and fitted with the activities going on in other spheres. These facts gave a snapshot of the area at the time of the debate.

Population growth had not, in relatively recent times, been seen as a problem. In fact, population had declined in the 1950s, and growth was not significant until the 1960s.

The number of boatyards had doubled in the 1950s and early 1960s. Norfolk was therefore attracting more business, presumably largely tourist-driven, even though the local population was declining for some of that time. This was not surprising as it correlated with the marketing effort being put in to the Broads holidays. However, apart from increased use of water frontage, this growth in boatyards had also not been seen as a problem.

That said, the 'Broads problem', he said, in terms of pollution, was perhaps down to holiday and recreation issues. There had been no serious pollution problem although some localised issues were related to sewage and agricultural waste.

The number of hire craft had quadrupled between 1945 and 1967. Two-thirds of all the hire firms and moorings were on the northern Broads, and the traffic on the northern rivers was three times that of the southern ones. This was probably because boats starting in the northern Broads tended to stay there, but those starting their cruises on the southern reaches, for some reason, tended to be more evenly distributed. Also, the overall recreational usage of the area, including private sailing and fishing, had grown rapidly in the 1950s and 1960s.

In the 1960s, the number of chalets for hire had doubled and the number of caravans had increased by 25 per cent. Although less than specific, there was a reference to this being a problem.

Much of this bears out the changes in holiday marketing and demographics. In some detailed points Shaw touched on an issue that is easy to overlook in this marriage of the holiday visitors to the Broads area, and it's inevitable that it came up in the discussion on planning. While a tiny percentage of planning applications for holiday accommodation were approved, virtually all applications for boat storage were approved. And one of the department's recommendations for investment had included parking. The increase in car ownership had made the Broads accessible to a wider audience, but when they got there they needed somewhere for the car while they were afloat.

Overall, two key factors emerged, and they were becoming familiar. The phosphates were a problem, within the main goal of conservation. And there was not enough cohesion in the authorities involved with the Broads.

One of those authorities was of course Broadland District Council, who stated at the outset that they saw two main areas where there was agreement. Firstly, it was accepted wholeheartedly that there was 'a problem' with the Broads. Secondly, any solution to the problem should be provided by local people, including district or county council personnel, rather than by people 'from away', with no local background or knowledge.

Fundamental to Broadland District Council's view were some more increasingly familiar concerns. There was no total harmony or cohesion. The districts did all agree on strategy, including that of National Park status. That National Park status as it stood did not offer enough power, especially given that pollution was such an issue.

In short, they were not in favour of a National Park, but interestingly, because they recognised both the problem and its urgency, they suggested pursuing the concept of the Broads being designated an Area of Outstanding Natural Beauty.

In a separate strand, Mr Mack, representing the council, posed a question that has an eerie resonance decades later. 'In a time of economic crisis,' he said, 'money is scarce. Whether it is money from ratepayers of Broadland, or taxpayers nationally, is it right to think of obtaining extra finance in the form of a 75 per cent grant from Central Government towards the creation and running of a new Authority when that 75 per cent still comes from public money albeit not from local ratepayers?' Like others, the council thought that the Anglian Water Authority should be a central force in cleaning up the Broads.

The Anglian Water Authority's response was positive. Admitting the phosphate problem, but pointing out the work they were doing, they made it plain that further research was needed and that they would 'meet their fair share of the cost'.

By the time the forum had reached a stage where the tourism industry could have its say, it was becoming obvious that not only was the 'Broads problem' a complicated one, it was a shifting one.

Several arguments were now emerging both within the University of East Anglia discussion group and beyond. The growth of tourism was having an impact on the Broads. On the positive side, it was generating wealth and employment for the region, but it brought controversy in both how it was affecting traditional life, with newer boat styles and more people flocking to what had been quiet areas, and in its contribution to what was now emerging as the main 'Broads problem' – the deteriorating environment.

In a way, the balance was shifting in that informed spokespeople were admitting that the boats and the tourists were by no means the sole culprits. Agriculture and sewage were, combined with some natural forces, also pushing the Broads towards an ecological and environmental crisis.

On top of that, there was a growing recognition that the Broads were suffering from a lack of cohesive management. Despite encouraging signs that the various parties, who on the face of it had differing goals, were displaying goodwill and some concerted work towards the common aim of protecting the area, the Broads were in free fall. And there was another trace element threading through the various opinions. Not quite universally held, but certainly prevalent, was the idea that if a cohesive form of Broads management could be found, and that it might possibly be through the National Park model, it should be handled by local people and not those 'from away'.

The common goals, and views, were touched on by Mr P. Naylor who, as director of the East Anglian Tourist Board, also contributed to the University of East Anglia Forum. Either by coincidence or intention he picked up the point made by the Norfolk Naturalists Trust. 'The object of nature conservation on the Broads,' he said, 'seems to be to manage a man-made landscape in the way twentieth-century man wishes to preserve it.'

His point was that the thriving tourist industry did not want to destroy its own 'product'. 'The tourists' interests and the nature conservation interests are totally tied up with each other and there is not too much difference between them.'

He went on to say, in a statement that needs some decoding from this distance in time, 'It has become clear that the object of conservation is as much to stop nature looking after its own, as it is to prevent man or tourist from spoiling a natural habitat.'

He drew his submission to a close by reiterating that the interests of tourism and conservation go hand in hand. Then, rather more positively, if controversially, he made some points that would bring him neatly to the now familiar refrain. Referring to a speech by the Port and Haven Commissioners, he said that their stance had appeared to be 'let's just carry on for ten years'. If that was the case, he asked, why had they come to the conference?

As to the Anglian Water Authority, their preparedness to pay their fair share was fine, but if they simply wanted to do some more research and 'see what happens', that was procrastination. In a slightly more apologetic tone he said that the existing bodies had 'done marvels', but they hadn't succeeded because they didn't have the powers.

The chairman of the Broads Society would echo much of this. They would support 'the scientists' because their work is vital. They would not support National Park status, *under current legislation*, because the Broads were unique and required a unique solution.

He made a valid point concerning the variety of the Broads however. It's a fascinating glimpse into the Broads holiday world of the time. There were, he said, and always would be, inevitable conflicts between the various activities, but the Broads could accommodate them all:

> Those who want their 'knees up' can go to Oulton Broad or Yarmouth. On a summer evening there are hardly any hire craft moored at Wroxham Broad; a few but a very few, fishing or bird watching. Yet a mile and a half down river at Salhouse Broad there are many. I do not know what the difference is, but it is a good thing because those who want to congregate go to Salhouse and those who want to be on their own can go to Wroxham or elsewhere. That is what we all want, because the Broads offer so much variety for so many and long may they do so.

There had been an allusion to the farming community in that they would have a problem, in the National Park format, with footpaths. Albeit legally entitled, people walking through working farmland was seen as a problem for the farmer. Mr Ritchie, of Hall Farm, Ludham, expanded on the agriculturalists' view. There was no doubt that they saw that there was a problem, and that a cohesive approach was needed. But in their view, that had to come from existing authorities. The Norfolk Branch of the National Farmers Union was strongly opposed to the Broads becoming a National Park. An Area of Outstanding Natural Beauty was equally unacceptable.

Neither of these models would benefit the farming community, they felt. There was no evidence from elsewhere in the country that it would. There would be problems obtaining permission for necessary farm buildings. The proposed park in Norfolk would be unique, but not in the way that other bodies had seen it. The NFU were clear that no other National Park included so much agricultural land. There would be restrictions on the farmer, and possible danger to the visitor.

Of course the natural habitat needed protecting, and yes, the growth in tourism was a mixed blessing, but as far as the NFU were concerned any problems could be sorted out by the existing bodies pulling together more.

All of this was of course the opinion of the various bodies involved. Invaluable as it was, and is in retrospect, to see how the great issues concerning Broadland evolved, it wasn't the voice of the general public.

At this point the consumer, or resident, had played a part in the story of the Broads in different ways. From way back, from the monks and marsh men to the boatbuilders and reed cutters, indeed even to the ancient workmen who had dug out the peat, unwittingly creating the Broads, they had trodden their paths through history, each leaving their mark. Now there was the late twentieth-century human, who was equally making an impression. It was arguably a more intrusive contribution to the condition of the Broads, but nonetheless it was born of work and labour. The only difference was the ever numerous tourist who, it now seemed, was not as exclusively guilty of the damage as first suspected. All of them had had their opinions and voices, some lost forever. The more recent ones were being recorded through research for marketing purposes. It was known what the tourist consumer wanted, because they were buying it.

But what of the local inhabitants? Aside from the councillors and the trusts, the water authorities and the scientists, what did local people think of what was happening to the Broads in the midst of this 1970s shift in awareness and planning for the future?

The Local View

Fortunately we have some insight as the result of a research programme carried out by the University of East Anglia School of Environmental Sciences at the time. Drawing on residents of the area around the rivers Bure and Thurne meant that the programme sought opinions from people who were likely to have been aware of scientific work, and press coverage of it, in the Barton and Hickling Broads areas.

Using a relatively sophisticated technique, the 'sample' were asked to rate the relative importance of issues, related to how much money they would be prepared to spend on them. In general people thought that nature conservancy was an important political priority 'even during the present harsh economic climate'. However there was less of a consensus over the question of whether funds for nature conservation should be cut back in line with reductions in public spending. Most disagreed with the view that spending on nature conservation should be reduced.

Next came the question that had been the subject of so much 'professional' debate. Did residents know much about the changes happening to Broadland vegetation in their area? It was accepted that the interviewees would have little detailed biological knowledge of 'eutrophication', or the change in vegetation resulting from nutrient enrichment. They were asked if they were aware of changes and then informed that nutrients were entering the water from sewage works at North Walsham and Stalham. Just over half the residents of North Walsham interviewed did not know that their treated sewage passed through Barton Broad; nearly three-quarters of Stalham residents interviewed were equally unaware. As to the sewage containing nutrients, 77 per cent of North Walsham residents and 81 per cent of Stalham residents were unaware of it.

Further probing revealed that this apparently interested group, living in a presumably aware area, were not fully informed of what the effects of this situation were. Once informed of 'eutrophication', they were concerned, and the phrase 'deterioration of the Broads' soon found its way into the discussion. However what they *perceived* as deterioration was dead fish, litter, debris and oil slicks. In reality the effect was much more to do with the decline of species such as water lilies, and the proliferation of algae, which leads to murky water. Only 3 per cent knew that.

If opinions on the National Park concept had been largely similar, but sharply defined where they differed, in the forum discussions and papers, the views and findings within the research sample were as muddy as the contaminated Broads. Put simply, there was very low awareness of what precisely a National Park was. Almost 60 per cent of the people were ambivalent. Just 20 per cent believed strongly that a National Park would do no good. A significant number did think that a National Park would provide better management, and that it would help control the environment. Overall there was a majority feeling that a park would cost more money, not really protect the ecology and that they were therefore 'against it'.

The researchers factored in to these findings that the interviewees had perhaps been influenced by press coverage, which they thought, or suggested, had not always been 'helpful'.

There was no doubt, though, and here there is a real resonance with the 'professionals', that these people wanted to see better and more effective management of Broadland.

The research then moved into a different gear. Proposing the idea of a fund to safeguard Broadland, both ecologically and for recreation, the interviewers found a 4-in-5 agreement to it. However, it seemed that a high moral tone soon crumbled when hard personal finances came into play. People who thought the fund was a good idea were not necessarily so keen to contribute to it if they lived in houses where their sewage was not treated. Admittedly these findings had to take account of people on low incomes, and the elderly who had a low level of interest in the future, but the fact was that an agreement with the *principle* of such a fund did not always match with having to pay for it, without direct *personal* benefit.

To simplify some of the findings, it was apparent that among an informed minority there was a willingness to do something about

129

preserving the Broads, and that overall people were prepared to make a financial contribution if they saw some direct, tangible benefit from it.

People also seemed to be aware of the various, largely voluntary, organisations who were doing their bit to lobby and influence government regarding conservation. Inevitably those who actively used the Broads for fishing and birdwatching were keener to see something done.

The picture was not a clear one. The recurrent feeling of the need for some more pulling together of resources was quite well established, but it was fair to say that while people were aware of the voluntary organisations there was little real knowledge of how successful, or not, they were.

The findings indicated that it might be time to appoint an executive officer who could educate the Norfolk population about the dangers of taking no action, and in so doing give added impetus to the work of the various voluntary bodies who were at least achieving something, albeit with modest resources.

It's also possible to look at some views expressed by other local residents at the time, to add more pieces to this jigsaw of opinions.

A Hoveton resident was not alone in having concern about farmers and landowners regarding the issue of footpaths. He felt that local control was biased in favour of farmers, who held many of the local council seats and thereby controlled access to the water.

This was rebutted by a local farmer from Ludham who said that, in his area at least, farmers did not close footpaths but encouraged walkers using the paths legally. Wandering through crops though was, understandably, a worry.

The soap powder manufacturers that Ted Ellis had mentioned were certainly in peoples' minds. This had a direct bearing on the phosphate question. Dr Moss, when questioned, talked about the American manufacturers. This was the 1970s, but the residual stigma of the great American consumer advertising boom of the 1950s was still very much in evidence. Soap powder manufacturers, led by America, had had an enormous sociological effect. They had delivered the money-off offers, free plastic flowers and indeed given the world, through sponsored TV drama, the 'Soap Opera'. They had also delivered what the consumer wanted, namely effective, 'whiter than white' results. As Dr Moss pointed out, the reason phosphates were used in detergents was that it was safe, worked well and consumers were pleased with it. The alternatives, including silicates and borates, were dangerous, especially to children.

Bringing his point to a close, he pointed out that the only workable solution would therefore be to go back to soap. Referring directly to America, he said that the detergent manufacturers there were now sensitive about their image, but the modern consumer now had the white, clean clothes they wanted, and to try and change the manufacturing process was not a realistic option. It was better to treat the phosphate at the sewage works.

As the second half of the 1970s developed, it would be realistic to say that there was a serious problem on the Norfolk Broads. They were deteriorating, and their future, in ecological terms, was precarious.

Tourism had certainly grown enormously and the relationship between the marketing of holidays on the Broads and the increased number of boats and people using them was inescapable. And yet this was by no means the sole cause of the problems. The debate had demonstrably shifted to the questions of farmers, phosphates and natural causes, with a lot of the concern over tourism being offset by the revenue it generated.

An absence of cohesive management of the Broads was emerging as a contributory factor in the slide towards a dangerous point of no return. There were obviously different, and differing, factions involved with the Broads, and in some cases there was more harmony and shared intent between them than was at first evident. Some kind of centralised control was needed, but this was Norfolk, and 'ill-informed' outsiders would not be welcomed to a position of management.

What was needed was locally driven, well-informed, proactive management with an understanding of all the various points of view but with the preservation of this unique wetland as its paramount objective. The question now was, who could do that? A significant factor in establishing the answer was the determination that powers would not be imposed on Norfolk, and in particular the Broads, from 'away'.

By the time the Countryside Commission, who had set in train research following the stalemate over the National Parks question some years earlier, had presented a paper and sought feedback from Norfolk, the options were becoming clearer.

In essence, to meet the increasingly urgent need for a solution there were four possible routes: to designate the Broads as a National Park under the current legislation; to designate the Broads as a National Park but with added legislative powers, especially over water quality and navigation; to establish a special Authority; or to give the Anglian Water Authority powers over navigation. Together, these four options seemed to embrace all of the various viewpoints and concerns that had been expressed up to that point, but there had to be a decision.

The Countryside Commission expressed a preference for a National Park with added powers. It also made comments about how it would work, presumably to quell the obvious concerns, and what it considered to be misconceptions. Such a park, it said, would not include large tracts of agricultural land. Neither would 'tourist publicity' be greatly increased. This was justified by saying that it was obvious that the Broads could not absorb endless numbers of visitors, although quite how it would be implemented was another question. Finally, and presumably trying to please everybody, it said that local people and councils would still have an input into the management; Norfolk opinion would not be ignored.

Further consultation, in what by now must have seemed an endless process, confirmed what had been emerging as opinion across many of those involved. A National Park under the current legislation had virtually no support. Giving the powers of navigation to the Anglian Water Authority was equally unpopular.

Many of the local conservation groups and trusts supported the idea of a park 'with added powers', as did a wider audience.

There was much detailed discussion about boundaries and farmland, and the planning issues concerning villages, but it was noticed that there was a considerable amount of interest in the option of establishing a special authority. In truth, the details of how such a body could be formed and run were sketchy, but the interest in it was real. So was the opinion of the Countryside Commission, who made it plain that they did not think it likely that the government would either finance it, or sanction transfer of such amounts of power to it, and away from the existing legislative bodies.

This was a critical moment. Looking back now, with the benefit of hindsight, it would appear that two profound issues came to the surface. Firstly, the Countryside Commission had underestimated the local opposition to a National Park, and to compound their error had perhaps assumed that Norfolk had not done its own research into the National Park model and found it wanting.

Secondly, they had grossly underestimated the less tangible but enormously important fact that this was Norfolk. It's where things were 'done different'. And it's not where control from outside, or 'being told what to do', sits easily.

Norfolk County Council had by now gone on record to say that it preferred a new option that had come from the Norfolk branch of the Association of District Councils. Steadfastly maintaining that no externally imposed authority was necessary, they had said that control over such profound issues needed to be held by existing organisations. Bringing the need for co-ordination back into focus, their proposal was the formation of a joint executive committee of the local authorities. It would have a Broads Officer, delegated powers and an administrative staff. It would have some local financing. It would be called the Broads Authority.

It would be ten years before further legislation created the Broads Authority in its present form. Before looking at its work and progress, it is appropriate to consider other events in the Broads story as the 1970s drew to a close.

Tourism in general within the area was booming. Hoseasons were able to report that they had exceeded all their targets for 1978.

This was in the face of the economic climate, which had remained difficult. If times were hard, people were prepared to find some fun, and holidaying in the UK was perceived as a sensible option when money was tight.

The season for Broads holidays had certainly extended in line with the national trend. The entire Hoseasons fleet of hire boats had been out during September, and half of it was booked out for October. This may not have been the overall picture as, in a press story at the time, Eric Humphries, then joint managing director at Hoseasons, referred to their performance as exceptional in the light of some 'other yards' having significant numbers of boats unlet during the season.

Hoseasons had sold 760,000 holidays in 1978. In a glimpse of the development of the brand, it's interesting to note that 260,000 of those had been boating holidays compared to 500,000 in holiday homes. Having achieved twenty-five weeks of bookings against a target of twenty-four, the company had, they said, obtained a booking record 'significantly above their nearest competitor'.

This performance had led to them believe that more boatyards would join them in the following year. Allowing for the obvious discretion in not naming the competitor, this was very much part of the PR battle to win the hearts and minds of the consumer and trade alike. Nonetheless, this was an outstanding performance for the company, who were by now a major force in the national self-catering holiday market.

It had been joint managing director Eric Humphries who had spoken to the press, but even now, as the company grew, James, or Jimmy, Hoseason was unquestionably a 'hands-on' manager. His ferocious attention to detail, dedication to embracing all that was happening in marketing and communication techniques, and relentless pursuit of excellence were evident throughout the organisation. Always pictured in the brochure, often with his customary pipe, he was not only the face of Hoseasons, he was the driving force.

It was the unnamed competitor who would stand up for Broadland and be quoted in the press very soon, though. David

Court spoke for the Norfolk and Suffolk Broads Yacht Owners' Association, or Blakes, when the Broads were dealt an unexpectedly harsh blow from forces close to home.

Anglia Television had produced a documentary in 1979 called *No Lullaby for Broadland*. The title was plainly a pun on either, or both, the song titles of 'Lullaby of Broadway' and 'Lullaby of Birdland'. Either way, it struck the wrong chord in Norfolk.

With the problems of the Broads' environment very much under discussion, and the fledgling Broads Authority now in place, this film showed the Norfolk Broads in a far-from-favourable light. Although some commented on the fact that it was good that Anglia Television had produced a film that had been shown across the network, and indeed that it had 'helped' by giving national coverage and therefore heightened awareness of the problems facing the Broads, the overriding reaction was that it simply wasn't fair.

David Court called it 'dishonest' and said that it 'underlined the lengths people are prepared to go to to make a sensational documentary'.

The elements that provoked the greatest reaction were 'telescopic' shots that created an impression of massively overcrowded boats and moorings at Horning, Wroxham and Potter Heigham. As well, in trying to communicate the problems of wildlife, the same shot of the same dead bird was shown eight times.

But what really caused anger was that the film seemed to show untreated human sewage being put into the water from motor cruisers. David Court said that that didn't happen.

The chairman of the Broads Consultative Committee said at their meeting, where again the exposure to the nation of the problem facing the Broads was accepted as beneficial, that, despite the furore, there had been no mention of the southern rivers and he expressed concern that the conservation issues had been focussed on in this way.

There was a call for a follow-up, a more 'serious' documentary. In the meantime, the curious mixture of national publicity and bad representation through questionable techniques had put the Broads and all its problems into the spotlight in a less-than-helpful way. Neither the conservationists nor the holiday industry were happy.

The year 1979 would bring another less-than-favourable Broads story to the public attention, albeit with a happy ending. On a Tuesday in June, the 63-foot *Queen of the Broads* had left Great Yarmouth for a two-hour river trip. It was a pleasant evening, and the 121 passengers, of all ages, were dressed in light summer clothing.

When the boat was overdue for her return, the alarm was raised and the inshore lifeboat *Waveney Forester* went out to find her. And find her they did.

The *Queen of the Broads* was stranded. In a sudden fog that had come down over Breydon Water, she'd run aground on a mud bank. It was eight hours before the passengers were transferred to a lifeboat, picking their way over the plank bridge put in place for them.

Muddy but unbowed, they returned to the Haven Bridge at Great Yarmouth praising the lifeboat crews and in good spirits. It had, though, been a salutary lesson. Firstly, there had been too many people out there to use the helicopter rescue service. Secondly, there had been no ship-to-shore radio. On a lighter note, although doubtless important at the time, there had been complaints about passengers having to pay for tea while stranded. In a serious vein it had shown that even experienced sailors can fall victim to the fog and hazards of Breydon Water. Norfolk does not have the cliffs and crashing waves of some of the UK's coastline, but, as in so many ways, it must never be underestimated.

In fact, only the previous year a spring tide had caused a huge wave to roar through Reedham, so that a barge hit the bridge and blocked the River Yare.

As the 1970s drew to a close, the battle for market share between the two big players in Broads holidays saw a confident Blakes predict a successful 1980s. With 1,200 Broads boats on their books, they'd sold 29,000 weeklong boat holidays in 1979, making it one of the best years in the company's history. Like Hoseasons, they had branched out nationally, and internationally. In fact, the Blakes fleet on the Broads had not grown at all since 1970; the growth was elsewhere, including France.

David Court said that it was now a matter of constantly raising standards to meet consumer demand as the self-catering holiday business continued to grow.

There was no doubt now as to where the Broads story had arrived. The balance between recreation and conservation had never been more finely pitched. Growing demand for holidays was good; it meant business. The Broads were not over their crisis of deterioration in terms of the environment. The holiday business was taking action over looking after the Broads, but there was still work to do. There was work to be done by other parties, as all the discussion groups and committees had shown. Not totally blameless, the boat-hire business was far from the only culprit in damaging the area.

However, boat hire had by now become a business of some considerable size. There had been a period of enormous growth, fuelled by many sociological factors, not least of which was the increase in holiday-time entitlement for many workers. The mention by Blakes that 1979 had been 'one of' the best years was, though, a valid point. The real growth had been earlier, and the peak of hire cruisers being available had been during the 1960s.

Even though there had been a levelling off of growth at the turn of the 1970s, into the 1980s there were still almost 100 businesses in Broads boat hire. Some of them were let by individual yards, of varying size, but the vast majority were by now let through either Blakes or Hoseasons, both of whom were now nationally recognised as significant holiday companies.

The much-quoted link between Broads tourism and commercial good for the region was evident by this time in the condition of the boatbuilding industry. Boats had always, traditionally, been built in Norfolk, but by the late 1970s the business was very strong. Its connection to the hire industry was undeniable. Not only was there a range of boats, from small dinghies to luxury cruisers, being built in Norfolk for use on the Broads, but craft designed and built there were being exported to other waterways in the UK, as well as France, where, of course, both Blakes and Hoseasons were expanding.

All of this meant employment. It was estimated that 800 people worked full-time in the boat-hire businesses at this point. On top of that, there were another 1,200 employed on a part-time basis providing the largely seasonal services, including cleaning and maintenance. But of course the holidaymakers bought in to the local economy, and that meant that the effect was more widespread. The staff in the pubs, cafés, restaurants and shops, not to mention the boating suppliers, gas suppliers, and even TV rental firms were all indirectly employed as a result of the boat-hire business. An estimate of 1979 put the true figure as between 5,000 and 6,000 people being involved. The Broads tourism industry was generating over £12 million in consumer spending in the region.

There was a paradox. While there was no restriction on the number of boats allowed on the Broads, opening the door for further expansion of this plainly viable market sector, the number of boats had in real terms fallen since the late 1960s. Certainly the data gathered for the 1967 Broads Plan showed more boats than there were in 1979. The picture was confused slightly by the fact that some yards had added boats, while others had either contracted or gone out of business.

The other factor to take in to consideration was that boating on the Broads had never been exclusive to hired boats. Private owners were an important part of the scene.

A glimpse at the figures for 1978 shows that there were 4,800 privately owned, motor-powered boats on the Broads, and 2,915 privately owned other craft, including 1,613 sailing boats, 1,275 rowing boats and 27 houseboats. That's a total of 7,718 compared to 6,110 in 1971. Of the 4,800 privately owned motorboats, only 2,047 were motor cruisers, the remainder being day launches, workboats and outboard dinghies.

As to hire boats in the same years, in 1978 there were 2,822 motor-powered boats and 1,079 in the other categories, making a total of 3,901 compared to 4,067 in 1971.

The reality was that although in the public debates it was often, if not usually, the holiday boats that were seen as the growing force, and the threat, it was actually the privately owned boats that were growing in number. Added to that was the question of the private owner who made short visits to the Broads, bringing a boat with them, often with one or more additional dinghies. All of these swelled the numbers and were difficult to control. The easily accessible and affordable licence was no real threat to the casual visitor. However, there were suspicions that, despite the best efforts of the authorities, some visitors paid no licence fee at all. Another factor was that private boat owners did not use the local shops and restaurants in the way that holidaymakers did.

The growth of privately owned boats was then an issue. It was suggested that off-river moorings would help ease traffic flow, and that a more rigorous policy on fees should be pursued.

If congestion was a problem, it wasn't entirely down to the number of boats. The Broads are particularly attractive as a boating holiday area because they have no locks, like the canals, and navigational challenges are few. However, they do have bridges. Wroxham and Potter Heigham, for example, could cause bottlenecks, and the issue of conservation embraced ancient crossings as much as wildlife. Preserve a bridge, or bypass it?

There may have been a plateau in hire-boat numbers but there was every reason to assume the business would grow. And with privately owned boats increasing in numbers, the Broads could only get busier.

1980–1990

A New Decade, A New Authority
As the 1980s arrived, there was work to do. The Broads Authority was now in place, but its arrival had not been straightforward. In the late 1970s, continued local resistance to powers being imposed on the region had resulted in the Countryside Commission having

to accept that the concept of the Broads Authority was the only way forward. It was, some said, a case of the Broads Authority having been formed less as a demonstration of the right way to go, and more as a result of refusing to be told by outsiders which way they should go.

Nonetheless, it was the route taken and it has had a profound effect on the history of the Broads. There would be several stages of development before the authority came finally and formally into being, and in the meantime there were some significant objectives set for it.

Those goals were to conserve and enhance the natural beauty and amenity of the area as a whole, including its wildlife, while protecting the economic and social interests of those who live and work in the area and preserving its natural resources. It was also necessary to facilitate the use of the Broads for recreational and holiday purposes both waterborne and land-based, and for the pursuit of scientific research, education and nature study.

In fairness, that did cover all the objectives of all the bodies involved, and contained the need to address the dichotomy of commerce and nature, science and leisure.

The fact was that there were some strings attached. These were that National Park designation would be put in place unless, by the end of 1978, there had been clear evidence that the authority had made clear progress in setting itself up, or if, by the end of 1980, having been set up, the authority had not made progress itself.

There were also clear instructions that a management plan had to be written, an annual report produced and acceptance of three Countryside Commission representatives as members of the authority. The authority also had to engage with the commission to establish the boundaries of the Broads. And there was the issue of agreeing on and writing the job description for, not to mention appointing, the all-important Broads Officer.

The late 1970s were days when there was less awareness of equal opportunities and of what would now be seen as sexist statements. The local press cannot therefore be blamed in retrospect for referring to the then yet-to-be-appointed Broads Officer as this 'hapless man'.

The comment came during the process of finding the right candidate for the Broads Officer position. Their point was that they saw the job as an impossible one. For how many people they spoke it's not known, but certainly the journalists must have been confident that they were echoing at least some local opinion, as well as expressing their own editorial comment. There is some justification in their argument, or at least it's possible to understand. It's one that will be familiar by now. The successful 'man', they said, would have to 'change everything for the better'. What's more, 'he' would have to 'reconcile the conflicting claims of naturalists, hire fleets, navigation, farmers and sportsmen'. He would have to create harmony between the 'jarring voices of a dozen or so local authorities'. In a final, stinging reflection, the *Eastern Daily Press* said that the Broads Officer would have to do all of that 'without offending anyone and without any clear brief as to what his priorities should be'.

Presumably, the required job description was actually couched in rather more positive and promising terms, as around 1,500 people applied for the post. Once more, however, the uniqueness of Norfolk, and the uncharted waters of the Broads Authority, would prove difficult for the 'outside world'. There is anecdotal evidence that some candidates who had been deemed acceptable subsequently refused to take up the position.

Undeterred, the authority continued to whittle down the choices. The proportion of men and women who applied is not known, but presumably they came from a range of private sector, academic and government backgrounds.

Eventually it was announced that the new Broads Officer would be Dr Aitken Clark.

Matthew Aitken Clark, a graduate in Architecture and Regional Planning from the London School of Economics, was born near Glasgow in 1936. He'd worked his way towards his degree by initially studying at night school. After graduating, he had worked in East Anglia, at Cambridge for a while, before joining the Greater London Council where he worked on planning and environmental studies. He went on to work abroad, in Italy and in the USA, becoming Professor and Head of Department for Regional Planning at South Carolina State University.

It was from the USA that he came back to Britain to take up the post with the Broads Authority in 1979. The long search for the right person was to prove worthwhile, as this skilled, diplomatic man, with all the relevant experience and a love of sailing, was everything the authority was looking for.

He in turn needed to look for a team as, odd though it sounds, on arrival he was in reality the only member of staff.

As Clark settled in to his role, the commercial fortunes of the Broads companies were as robust as had been predicted for the start of the 1980s. Just as Blakes had done, Hoseasons were now selling boating holidays in France. At home the company was forging ahead. The office systems and increased use of technology were enhancing the booking process, and the advertising strategy was continuing to use a mixture of press and TV.

All important still was the brochure. This was the ultimate 'shop window' from which holidays were chosen. An increase in the number of brochures printed could be a barometer of success, in that it confirmed demand. But it was how the brochures got to the public that mattered. Already using 'Dial-A-Brochure' and still sending out brochures in response to press advertising, Hoseasons continued to explore additional channels of distribution to increase market share and sales. By 1985, they were printing 2 million copies of their brochure and, for the first time, expanding distribution of it by the innovative means of making it available through high-street travel agents.

Another business with an important role in the history of Broadland was also changing and growing. If further evidence were needed to prove the claims that tourism on the Broads was good for local business then it was amply provided by Roys of Wroxham.

The company had come a long way since their early days. Such was their connection to the Broads business that by 1931 they had moved their headquarters to Wroxham.

They too were aware of the power of the brochure, and had built up a significant 'mail-order' business by distributing a 300-page brochure through the boat-hire companies, forging ever closer their links to the Broads.

Way ahead of the other players, they had also achieved national recognition. Arnold Roy had become something of a radio celebrity back in 1938 when he appeared on the hugely popular show *In Town Tonight*. Presented as the man from the 'World's largest Village Store', this was a master stroke of publicity. Broadcast nationally, the show was heard by people who had holidayed in Norfolk and knew the Broads, and the shop. The uninitiated were intrigued. Brand awareness of Roys went off the scale.

There had been some challenging times for the company in the 1950s, which were a setback given its previous growth and its having weathered the war as well as any business did. The 1960s saw a return to calmer waters. Despite some troubled times, this world-famous business was, by the 1980s, a huge, modern store, sporting a dozen checkouts. For generations of people Roys of Wroxham is an integral part of their Norfolk Broads holiday memories.

The Crisis at Halvergate

Less likely to feature in their recollections was the area of marshland at Halvergate. Much more a part of the old, traditional Broadland landscape, these marshes had for years been less involved with the development of tourism, and more a marriage of two other elements in the countryside's make-up. Old-school agriculture and diverse wildlife and vegetation had coexisted, drained by pumps manned by marsh men. It was the Broadland scene in aspic.

Of all the bodies, groups and organisations that have played their part in the history of Broadland, and there has been much evidence of their number and differing needs and aims, there are some that have not hitherto made the headlines or said their piece as forcibly as others. One such is the Lower Bure, Halvergate Fleet and Acle Marshes Internal Drainage Board.

In 1980 they were to become the catalyst for a situation that would make even the *Eastern Daily Press*' description of the newly arrived Aitken Clark's job sound realistic.

Halvergate Marshes had been traditionally used for grazing. This was how agriculture and wildlife worked together in these flat lands. As idyllic as it was, it was decreasingly profitable. The shift towards arable farming had therefore begun, seemingly with little notice being taken, even though it had had an impact on the ecology. Access was difficult, too, so road construction and farm equipment had made their mark.

Now, the Lower Bure, Halvergate Fleet and Acle Marshes Internal Drainage Board wanted to convert Halvergate Marshes to arable farming. To start the process they submitted the necessary forms to the Ministry of Agriculture asking for a grant. The grant was to cover new pumps, drainage work and road building. It would affect around 5,000 acres.

Neither the process nor conversion work of this type was unprecedented. What was new was a Ministry of Agriculture policy to advise local authorities of intentions to, and applications for, land drainage.

The new policy therefore meant that the Drainage Board had to contact and consult with the new Broads Authority. This looked very much like a first and demanding test for the much-desired cohesive and central management organisation. Here was commerce, in the form of ancient agriculture as opposed to relatively new boat hire, engaging with nature, conservation and change. It was farmers' livelihoods that were in question.

The Broads Authority objected to the request. This meant that the grant was not forthcoming. Negotiations began. It was a complicated situation. For a start, the new Broads Authority had farmers among its members, and diplomacy would be needed as the National Farmers' Union was staunchly behind the Drainage Board. Added to that was the financial problem that could develop.

If refused the right to convert to arable, the farmers involved would want compensation.

There were protracted discussions. The tone varied from amicable to acrimonious as agreements were nearly reached, then fell apart. The Countryside Commission was involved and they, increasingly exasperated, called for a public inquiry.

There was an irony here too. So many times Norfolk had gone against the grain, insisting that management of the Broads should be from a local perspective, as opposed to national government policy. Now, the government were insistent that the solution be found locally.

It didn't happen. Out of the blue, because none of the stalemated parties were consulted, the government implemented Section 48 of the Wildlife and Countryside Act. In doing so, they agreed to finance some new pumps but then drew a line as to the rest of the grant.

Initially this appeared to be a brave move. It was the first time that grant aid had not been forthcoming because conservation had been deemed to take precedence over agriculture.

Somehow, though, it felt as if it wasn't over, and that there were some loose ends blowing around in the winds across the marshes.

Not all visitors to Broadland are holidaymakers. In late 1980, the Broads Authority were called on by the Countryside Commission. This was part of the setting-up arrangements and not unexpected. Had the authority made sufficient progress or was National Park designation now imminent? The answers were quite positive. It was deemed that there had been progress, and that the authority had established itself as a viable entity. Park status would not be insisted on, and indeed support would continue. While the compliments were tempered with some concerns over there not being an annual report published, and a delay in the production of a management plan, allowances were made for their being so few staff.

Interestingly, given the staunchly independent stance taken by Norfolk in the original discussions, it was noted that the experience gained in the region would now be of use when the government were talking to other areas where National Park status was in question.

With the future of Broadland so much in focus, it was the 1980s that suddenly produced a fascinating throwback to its very beginnings. At Acle, in the great flat expanse towards Great Yarmouth, a cache of Roman coins was unearthed. Acle had been an important port in Saxon times, and it was situated in lands that had emerged from the sea. Even though the Roman occupation of the area was well documented, this sudden peek into the civilised society that had been so involved in digging out the peat that formed the Broads was a timely reminder of the region's origins.

The 1980s was also an important time for two organisations that capture the history of the Broads and allow a valuable insight into their natural and working past.

In 1981, the Norfolk Wherry Trust was able to commence work on the wherry base at Womack Water, near Ludham, on land and water frontage leased from Norfolk County Council. This was an important stage in the journey that has led to the preservation and continued use of the Norfolk Broads' most famous wherry.

A dedicated band of local people had first got together in the late 1940s to discuss a plan to ensure that at least one wherry would be preserved. These were the days when cargo had been shifted to train and lorry. It's extraordinary to realise now that some of these noble craft, essential to the history of the Broads, were simply sinking, in some cases literally, into oblivion.

Events moved quite quickly. Following the meeting, a letter was published in the *Eastern Daily Press* in February 1949 suggesting that a trust be formed with the aim of preserving a wherry. By 23 February there was an open meeting in Norwich's Stuart Hall. By the time it closed, a trust had been proposed and agreed, and over £500 had been raised. The elected chairman of the new trust was Mr Humphrey Boardman, who had formally proposed its formation.

Someone else there that night was Roy Clark. It was his bookshop on Tombland in Norwich where that first discussion had taken place. Now elected as one of the trust's first trustees, he eloquently summed up their aims.

'We visualise,' he said, 'a live, active vessel, plying the waters and on which the younger generation can set their feet and learn something of the sort of life, the sort of craft and the sort of men who raised our city and county to its current standing.'

To do that, though, meant that they needed a wherry to preserve. There was an initial suggestion to build a new one. This was not as odd as it sounds. A new craft would allow them to meet Roy Clark's beautifully expressed objectives. Next came the idea of refitting an old, existing boat. A sunken craft appeared to be available but the costs of working on her proved to be prohibitive.

Then came a development. Moored in Norwich near Carrow Bridge, by the Colman's mustard factory works, bereft of her mast, was a fifty-year-old wherry called *Plane*. Lady Mayhew, who was a passionate supporter of the trust from the outset and was at the Stuart Hall meeting, was a member of the Colman family. Her influence helped in transferring the wherry to the trust.

Work began straight away, and it was with considerable relief that the hull of the boat was discovered to be sound.

Just over £1,000 was spent on restoring the *Plane*. By October 1949, she was ready for work. Before her 'maiden' voyage, from Great Yarmouth to Norwich, there had been one other job to do. That was to change her name. She had not always been called *Plane*. Her name would now be her original one, and it would live on as a testament to those who believed in saving a wherry. When she sailed on 11 October 1949, she was *Albion*.

Albion went straight to work. Within a year she'd covered over 2,000 miles and she'd carried cargo. Her journeys echoed the trading so typical of a bygone era. In her 'first life' she had sailed, under skipper Jimmy Lacey, from Lowestoft to Bungay carrying coal at a shilling a ton. Now she carried timber, grain and sugar beet between Norwich, Surlingham and Cantley. Unique when she was built, in 1898, because of her 'carvel' construction and green-and-oxide colours, she was unique again. A trading wherry when all the others had gone. She worked ceaselessly until 1952, but by then the old problem had recurred. It was difficult to find cargo. The competition was too much.

In 1953, *Albion* crossed a boundary from the cargo and commerce of her trade and almost became part of the boat-hire business. With work still patchy, she was cleaned out and chartered out. Boy Scout groups often took her, sleeping in hammocks in the cargo freehold.

It would set a precedent. The wherry had almost sunk on two occasions and her upkeep was proving financially demanding. From the early 1960s she carried only people, never again to have a hold full of cargo.

Her role changed, but her importance grew. *Albion* is world-famous, and decades after those first inspirational meetings the aims of the trust are met every day. The great 'black-sailed traders' of the Norfolk Broads will never be forgotten.

Just as the Norfolk Wherry Trust has kept alive such a vital part of the Broads' commercial history, another group has done so much to preserve the natural habitat and traditions. Just two years after the wherry base was begun at Womack Water, it seemed that another era was ending when, for financial reasons, Norfolk County Council's education centre at How Hill was closed.

It was 1983 and the centre had been open for seventeen years. The property dated back to the early twentieth century, when the Norwich architect Edward Boardman had bought the 800 acres of land. It was Edward's son, Humphrey, who would play such a role in the life of *Albion*.

In 1904, Edward built a house for himself on an unusually high piece of ground, overlooking the marshland by the River Ant. At first it was little used, being mainly a holiday home. In 1915, however, he extended the place considerably and it became the family's home. The house itself was imposing but the gardens he planted were magnificent. A formal garden, complete with topiary, was complemented by 'secret gardens' with ponds and flowers, as well as exotic shrubs and rare trees. Edward Boardman planted 70,000 trees in all at How Hill.

Boardman died in 1950 (so presumably saw the *Albion* restored) and his estate was complicated by the lands being divided. In 1966, Norfolk County Council bought the house and the surrounding marshes and woodland. There, until 1983, the council's education department ran an education centre. Then came the problems that caused it to be closed.

The closure was not popular. A public campaign was needed before a solution was found. The Norwich Union Insurance Group, as it was in the pre-Aviva days, led a consortium to rescue the centre. Anxious to help, the still-new Broads Authority was an active partner with Norwich Union in setting up the How Hill Trust in 1984. Norwich Union leased the property to the trust until handing over the freehold in 2002.

The How Hill Trust now provides an ideal location for courses and conferences, and delivers exceptional environmental education for children and young people on residential field courses. All of the issues that have flowed through this story of the Broads are there to be learned about at this unique place. The changes to the environment, the habitat, the quality of the water and the impact of tourism are all taught and explained in the very heart of a truly Broadland setting. The house is now Grade II listed and the 90 hectares of marshland are a Site of Special Scientific Interest (SSSI). Among the treasures of the place is Toad Hole Cottage, a realistic reconstruction of a marsh man's home. It is almost the entire Broads landscape and challenges in miniature.

On the wider canvas, the Broads Authority was busy on matters aside from its valuable contribution to How Hill. The loose ends at Halvergate needed tidying up. Farmers were still pressing for land to be converted to arable use. There were serious financial implications for the authority if the conversions were halted and compensation sought.

Once again there were lengthy, and often stalled, negotiations. This time, though, the tone was more acrimonious. It got physical. There were demonstrations by Friends of the Earth, who stood in the way of tractors and equipment and grabbed national media exposure for doing so. A Mr Wright who farmed there had, through the machinations of the legal discussions, found himself, in effect, permitted to plough. The demonstration in front of his equipment daunted him and he stopped, saying that he would settle for the authority's previous offer, which he had declined. When the Broads Authority would go no further than that original offer Mr Wright prepared again to plough. And the Friends of the Earth prepared again to stop him.

It was a mess. The government were becoming increasingly anxious about the national and political implications. The authority was worried about losing the habitat to arable farming, and, realistically, the possible financial implications of compensation if it wasn't converted to arable use. They were now in a potentially vulnerable position. It was a case of failure not being an option for them, and financial loss not being an option for the farmers. All of this was going on under the watchful eyes of the Countryside Commission.

The negotiations and legal machinations continued throughout 1984 and in to 1985, when it was the Countryside Commission who found a way through. The plan involved some careful interpretation of legal requirements. There was a bigger picture to consider as these were the days of the controversial Common Agricultural Policy, making this an international issue. The point was that those who opposed the farmers in their attempts to turn traditional grazing land into arable farms saw the shift as not only a conservation issue but one driven by the chance to make a profit from selling grain that might never find its way to market. Many were the stories of vast quantities of crop doing nothing other than contributing to what was called the 'EEC grain mountain'.

The solution came in the form of the highly innovative and historically important Broads Grazing Marshes Conservation Scheme. In an unprecedented move, it was made possible to pay farmers compensation of £50 per acre if they allowed their land to continue to be used for grazing. Such was the complexity of the plan that it involved the government setting the European precedent for the establishment of Environmentally Sensitive Areas.

Not only did the farmers take up the offer in greater numbers than expected but, because the land met the criteria, the Norfolk Broads became an Environmentally Sensitive Area (ESA) in 1986. There had been many parties involved, and it had taken time, but the result boded well for conservation, and the Broads Authority.

If the winds of change were blowing in the politics of Broadland, it was a natural force that would wreak havoc in the following year. The great storm of October 1987 hit Norfolk and the Broads as it did everywhere. Gorleston in Norfolk, near Great Yarmouth, is estimated to have had the highest-speed gust in the UK, blasting in at 122 mph. Trees were uprooted, buildings damaged and of course boats were vulnerable. Many that were moored broke away, only to be damaged by falling trees. Power loss was a serious problem in Norfolk, with so much repair work needed that the Eastern Electricity Board, as it then was, had to draft in engineers from other parts of the country.

Nature had seemingly sent a stern reminder that whatever agenda man was working on, there are forces greater than any he can muster.

As the year turned, so too did the story of the Norfolk Broads. The year 1988 was vital in the region's history. It had been ten years since the prototype Broads Authority had come into being, and it had plainly passed the initial goals it had been set. National Park status had not been imposed on the Broads by the government and there seemed little doubt that the case was proven for a single statutory body of management. The Broads Authority was working.

The way forward lay in the Broads Bill. The course of this piece of legislation proved to be considerably more difficult to navigate than the waterways themselves. In 1982, the Broads Authority had published their management plan in the form of a document entitled 'What Future for Broadland?' This plan returned to some familiar waters. While ambitious in setting out a substantial list of objectives, it displayed some nervousness over the financial and manpower resources available to meet them, making it plain that all of the various bodies involved in the Broads needed to do their bit.

High on the list of participating organisations was the Anglian Water Authority, whom the Broads Authority saw as the key players in maintaining water quality. An essential issue in the conservation debate, the condition of the water, now a major concern, would be helped enormously if the sewage problem was controlled.

Over the next two years the question of how the Broads would continue to be managed wore on. By 1984, it was inevitable that there needed to be some form of statutory legislation to create a formal new authority, given that there was a blueprint for it in existence. Furthermore, the prototype seemed to be working and it was unlikely that any other option would garner as much support or favourable public opinion.

Norfolk County Council was charged with raising a Bill for parliament. It was a lengthy and complex process, becoming derailed in 1985 when the council, after having done much preparatory work, were advised that the legislation they were proposing fell short of parliamentary requirements to be a Private Bill.

It was a blow, but not the end of the road. The government had little option but to frame the legislation itself. The purpose was the same. When it came down to it, the Broads Authority as it then stood needed to be formally established with a definite future and some real powers and objectives. It would be over a year before all the twists and turns had been negotiated and the Broads Bill became law in 1988.

As a result of yet more legal and constitutional matters, the Broads Authority did not officially come into being until April 1989; the fact was that there now existed a body charged with the management of the Broads. They were given some specific responsibilities. As they stand today, those responsibilities are worded almost exactly as they were in the period when the various stages of the Bill were being debated.

As a result of the Norfolk and Suffolk Broads Act 1988, the Broads Authority is a Special Statutory Authority. In effect very similar to those of the English National Parks Authority, its responsibilities are conserving and enhancing the natural beauty, wildlife and cultural heritage of the Broads; promoting opportunities for the understanding and enjoyment of the special qualities of the Broads by the public; and protecting the interests of navigation while having regard to the national importance of the Broads as an area of natural beauty and one which affords opportunities for open-air recreation. Further consideration was required for the desirability of protecting the natural resources of the Broads from damage and the needs of agriculture and forestry, as well as protecting the economic and social interests of those who live or work in the Broads.

With its organisation and constitution in place, the Broads Authority officially appointed Dr Aitken Clark as its chief executive. In the conservation arena, he would be active over and above this role. From 1990 to 1996 he was president of the Europarc Federation, where he played an important part in European National Parks, as well as serving in several other international conservation organisations.

1990–2000

It was also during the 1990s that he was instrumental in another major project within Broadland. It was in 1995 that work really got underway for the restoration of Barton Broad. One of the largest Broads, Barton had been a worry for years. In the 1970s, the sewage problem had caused it to be virtually devoid of aquatic plants and barely able to sustain fish.

Although improvements in sewage treatment at that time had enhanced water quality, there was still a considerable amount of nutrients trapped in the mud on the bottom. Barton Broad was silted up to the point where it was too shallow for boats. By 1992, it was evident that something had to be done and planning was commenced. The size of the task soon became apparent. Whether or not the long-term effects would be sufficient, it was essential to pump out around 300,000 cubic metres of the mud and the phosphates it contained. Contractors were consulted and appointed to carry out a truly massive operation.

300,000 cubic feet of mud coming out of the Broad was one thing; what to do with it was another. In a process that would take four years, the mud was pumped out and placed into what were called 'settlement lagoons' covering 22 hectares of adjacent fields. There it was left to dry. Contained by banks built from the topsoil, the mud slowly settled and, as it dried, the water found its way back to the Broad. When it did, it was cleaner because the phosphates had 'stuck' to the silt particles, remaining behind.

It was a significant feat of engineering. Working all but ceaselessly for those four years, the great pump inched its way across the Broad, depositing the mud day after day. The results were encouraging. By 1998 it was evident that the drying mud was developing a stable soil structure capable of sustaining root growth. And it was proved to be so. Crops have been successfully grown there since. The entire project, known as 'Clearwater 2000', represented some £3 million of investment and it resulted in Barton Broad returning to its former glory. The conservation benefits were the return of wildlife, including rare plants, and otters. As for recreation, Barton would become one of the most popular areas for holidaymakers, sailors and anglers.

In a completely unrelated twist in the history of Broadland, and Barton, 1995 saw a crime committed that had a curious link to the area's past. A portrait, *Miss Nelson*, had been hung at Barton Rectory. It had been there for some years, having originally been sited at Cobb Hall in Yaxley. Since the 1850s it seemed that wherever the painting was, so too was the ghost of Miss Nelson. When the picture was bought by the owner of Barton Rectory, the spirit came with it. However, in 1995 the painting was stolen, not to be seen again. Interestingly, the ghost disappeared too.

A less 'spooky' glimpse back into Broads history came to light in the 1990s. The yacht *Zoe* had been assumed to be the oldest hire boat on the Broads, her hull having been discovered in 1945. She was restored, and although her design put her as a craft of the early twentieth century there seemed to be no trace of her prior to the Second World War.

A Mr Barnes of the Norfolk Broads Yachting Company decided to research *Zoe* and although the Broads Authority, whose records didn't go back far enough, couldn't help, some old holiday brochures could. In the early Blakes brochures, where yachts were described in considerable nautical detail, he found her. *Zoe* had changed her name. Originally she'd been named *Jubilee*, and for a very good reason. The Ernest Collins yard had built her in 1896 and named her for Queen Victoria's Diamond Jubilee. Here was a craft that was a wonderful link to the emergence of boating for pleasure on the Norfolk Broads.

The 1990s also saw two significant events in the Hoseasons story. At the start of the decade, James Hoseason had been made an OBE for services to tourism. By the end of the decade he'd retired. His credentials sum up his huge involvement with the Broads. A Fellow of the Chartered Institute of Marketing, he was also a member of the English Tourist Board and had been a founder of the Tourism Society. These great passions for the area, the business and the innovative and successful marketing of it had seen Hoseasons grow from those first days of the 1940s to a company selling around £100 million of holidays a year. Thousands were employed directly at the company and indirectly across the boatyards and holiday sites. Hundreds of thousands took a Hoseasons Holiday every year.

As the twentieth century drew to a close, another development would produce that most unexpected arrival: two new Broads. Just 2 miles east of Norwich, at Whitlingham, gravel was being extracted. It was to have many uses in the rapidly altering centre of Norwich. The new 'Forum' building, containing the library, which would replace the previous one lost in a fire, the Castle Mall shopping centre and subsequently the Chapelfield shopping area all needed the material.

The work on extracting the gravel had begun in 1990. In an echo of the peat diggings from so long before, the resultant 'quarries' would be flooded to create firstly Whitlingham Little Broad and eventually, in 1995, Whitlingham Great Broad.

The area has become a 'Country Park', and is not only a haven for wildlife but a hugely popular spot for visitors. It's home to the Whitlingham Outdoor Centre, which was funded by the National Lottery and Sport England and is run by Norfolk County Council.

Another twentieth-century Broad is the one at the University of East Anglia. It too is the result of quarrying and today supports a huge range of wildlife.

Hoseasons would neatly close one century and open another with continued innovation. In 1999 they became the first UK holidays to be booked directly online. By 2001, the company had its first totally interactive website.

Norwich: The City by the Broads

The University of East Anglia is, in historic terms, a relatively new institution. It was created in Norwich in the 1960s. The city itself has a much longer history, and an important one. From the Middle Ages to the great changes brought about by the Industrial Revolution it was England's second city, bowing only to London in importance.

Most visitors to the Broads will go to Norwich. An ancient city, Norwich is today as inextricably linked to the Broads as it ever was. The very origins of the Norfolk Broads can be traced to the peat diggings of the Middle Ages; when the monasteries excavated the peat for fuel, Norwich was their biggest customer. The cathedral alone is estimated to have consumed over 300,000 tonnes of it a year.

In the nineteenth century it was the merchants in Norwich who, recognising the problems encountered by commercial shipping on Breydon Water, began to formulate a plan to improve the waterways between the city and the sea.

Still standing proudly on the city's skyline is the cathedral spire, built by the Normans who themselves had worked with the peat of the Broads. Directly beneath the cathedral and retaining its ecclesiastical name is Bishop's Bridge. This is the limit for navigation for hire craft on the Norfolk Broads.

Just before the bridge is Norwich yacht station, an essential part of Broads history and where 'sailors' have moored during their Norfolk holiday for over a century. It was near here, on the River Wensum, that Broads pioneer John Loynes built and sailed boats before moving to Wroxham to become a catalyst in the boat-hire business.

Across the bridge from the yacht station is Norwich railway station. This wonderful Victorian building was at the centre of the railway boom that made the Broads so much more accessible during the nineteenth century, and again in the mid-twentieth century with the post-war expansion in holidays. The opening of that quintessential Broads story, Arthur Ransome's *Coot Club* is set on this station.

The line from Norwich, out into the Broads via Brundall, was the scene of what for many years was Britain's worst-ever rail disaster. Twenty-five people were killed and seventy-five injured in the head-on collision that would become known as the Thorpe Railway Disaster.

The Norwich School of Painters, working from studios in the city centre and by the Wensum, would make the Broads a favourite subject, propelling the area into art history and the world's imagination.

The weavers and textile workers of Norwich were among the first to seize on the river as a place of recreation, and the Water Frolics at Thorpe in the 1820s are some of the earliest manifestations of regular 'holiday' activity on the Wensum.

In more modern times the 'politics' of the Broads have often been centred in Norwich. Norfolk County Council and the Broads Authority are based there to this day. It was in the city centre that meetings such as the one to create the Norfolk Wherry Trust were held.

Changed by the shift from manufacturing to a largely finance and commercial centre, Norwich is a place of enormous historic interest, boasting some of the finest streets, museums and ancient buildings in the country. Since the Broads became a holiday destination, Norwich has proudly associated itself with its rural neighbours and welcomed thousands of visitors who see it as a central point in a Broads trip.

7

The Twenty-First Century

In the great history of the Broads, the arrival the twenty-first century was but a small step. To look at Broadland at the start of the new millennium it's appropriate to restate how the area is defined. In terms of the Broads Authority's remit, the borders are fixed around the 'flood plains and lower reaches of the rivers Bure, Yare and Waveney and their tributaries, the Thurne, Ant, Wensum and Chet'. This is known as the authority's 'executive' boundary.

Although the region obviously spreads further, taking in the urban areas of Norwich and Great Yarmouth, for example, there are some ninety-three parishes within the 'executive' area. The fact that, in 2001, of the 2,550 households in that 'executive' area some 466 were 'holiday or second' homes, is an indication of how important tourism is to Broadland. This shift, taking over a century, had perhaps contributed to the negative effect of the scarcity of affordable housing for local residents, but it had not eradicated the traditional crafts such as thatching and reed cutting, which still formed a small but important part of the local economy. For all its importance, though, in reality the Broads boat-hire business had been shrinking. The 855 motor cruisers licensed for hire on the Broads in 2009 might seem a small number compared to the almost 2,000 in the 1978 statistics, but it was an increase after what was perceived as the real low point: 2008.

What had shown real growth was the number of privately owned motor cruisers. In 2009, there were 4,746 on the Broads; the 1978 figures had shown 2,047.

Despite some fluctuation, the Broads boat-hire business had grown continuously since the nineteenth century. The increases in mobility brought first by the railways and then the car had made the Broads accessible. The post-war increase in holiday time and the relationship between consumers and marketing had produced the growth of the 1960s. But, when once newfound affluence had brought more people to boat *hire*, now it seemed that, despite the swings in the national economy, the more recent increases in affluence had produced more boat *owners*.

On the face of it this had to be good news for the Broads. Closer examination, however, revealed that this was not as straightforward as it appeared. In another example of how some sociological factors constantly repeat themselves throughout the story, there was now another demographic distinction appearing. Holidaymakers engaged with the Broads at many levels. By definition a holiday meant exploring the area, visiting the cafés, shops and pubs around Broadland and, in short, spending money with local businesses. Those who owned boats, either having them moored in Norfolk or cruising to the county, did not behave in the same way. Often loading up with supplies before they set off from home, and then remaining determinedly self-contained when they arrived, these visitors did not necessarily mean income to Broads-based establishments.

In overall terms, the 2000s can be said to be a period when different sensibilities were apparent. It was a changing and complex picture. There was a pronounced north–south divide in Broads activity. Some boatyards had not survived the downturn and the resultant sales and acquisitions meant that the hire fleets had moved around. There were now some seventeen yards operating in the northern sector of the Broads, with just seven in the south. Almost a third of that total hired their boats entirely, or in part, through either Hoseasons or Blakes. An increase in bigger, more luxurious boats met some tastes, but reduced mobility, with these sizeable craft not always being able to negotiate all the bridges.

The overall reduction in the size of the hire fleets was, however, coincident with an increase in the quality of the product. The change in sensibilities is best demonstrated by two factors. Firstly, by now there was a marked increase in an almost retrospective appeal for Broads holidays. Traditional 'half-decker' boats and cabin yachts were in demand as people wanted a return to the 'camping under sail' appeal of exploring the Broads.

Important in this area was the Norfolk Heritage Fleet Trust. Based at Hunters Yard in Ludham, this organisation has an interesting and quintessential Broads story. Working from traditional timber-built Broads boat sheds of 1930s origin, the yard had operated independently up to 1968. It was then sold to Norfolk County Council, who renamed it the Norfolk County Sailing Base. They upheld the traditions of the yard but directed much of its efforts into encouraging young people to discover sailing and the Broads. Mid-1990s economies meant that the council put the Sailing Base up for sale. A campaign produced some £100,000 from public sources and a subsequent £200,000 from the Heritage Lottery Fund. The result was the establishment of the Norfolk Heritage Fleet, who took over Hunters Yard. The encouragement of young sailors remained a vital objective but, chiming precisely with the mood of the times, so too did hiring the boats to those wishing to cruise the Broads in traditional style.

Maintained by experts, the fleet of 1930s boats are the very essence of Broads tradition. So much so that one of them, *Lullaby*, was to find fame in another twist of Broads history that reflected their timeless appeal. In an arguably odd move, the BBC decided to dramatise two of the Arthur Ransome books set on the Broads, combining *Coot Club* and *The Big Six* into one and calling it *Swallows and Amazons Forever*. The series came out in the 1980s, and when it did the legendary yacht in the books, *Teasel*, was 'played' by none other than the Heritage Fleet's *Lullaby*.

161

Such was the resurgence of interest in the period, the place and the boats caused by the series that, in a similarly bizarre move, the publishers of Ransome's books put out the almost exactly, yet definitely differently, entitled book, *Swallows and Amazons for Ever!*

Such is the authenticity of these 1930s boats that they have no electric power. It's oil lamps and gas cookers that fuel the feeling of days gone by. And this is sailing. They also have no engines.

If the nostalgic appeal was the first of the new sensibilities, then the absence of an engine matched exactly the second one. Over and above the informed and active experts, people in general were now much more aware of the need for a 'greener', conservation-oriented approach towards a sustainable philosophy for the Broads.

By 2006, a strategy for sustainable tourism had been produced. The Broads Authority was quite clear about what this relatively new concept meant. Sustainable tourism was, they said, 'responsible tourism'. It was tourism that took into account 'the needs of the environment, local residents, local businesses and visitors now and in the future'. Unarguably correct, these objectives had, and have, to be put into the context of the size of the challenge. Tourism is a driving force, an essential ingredient, in the economy of the Broads, and eastern England. Even accounting for the 'self-contained' boat owners, visitors are vital. By the early twenty-first century, and certainly by 2009, more than 7 million visitors a year were going to the Broads. Their expenditure of almost £420 million was supporting over 6,000 jobs. Over 120 years after Davies had published his guide to the Broads, complete with an advertisement from Loynes' boatyard, the balance between the waterways' quiet, unspoiled charm and their use as a profitable recreational destination was still, and perhaps more than ever, precarious to say the least.

This is a good point, then, to examine what was happening in the relationship between man and nature in early twenty-first-century Broadland. In the natural world, water quality had improved considerably over a period of almost thirty years. This was the result of positive action by the boat-hire companies, sewage treatment involving the water companies and changes in agricultural practice by farmers.

With water quality very much in mind, as well as the wider issues of fuel shortages and global warming, The Broads Authority and some boatyards worked together in 2006 on an interesting experiment.

Eight yards were involved: Alexander Cruisers and Silverline Marine from Brundall; Barnes Brinkcraft and Sabena Marine from Hoveton; Woods Dyke from Horning; Faircraft Loynes from Wroxham; City Boats from Thorpe; and Connoisseur Cruisers. The two-year test was funded by the Broads Authority's Sustainable Development Fund and carried out by the yards. The overall objective was to encourage the use of cleaner sources of fuel; the test was to use biodiesel and electric boats to obtain a comparison with conventional means of propulsion.

The authority was obviously enthusiastic to pursue such an experiment. So too were the boatyards. Keen to lead the field in better practice, this could be the dream ticket. If there was a fuel that was cheap to use as well as being environmentally friendly, then everyone was a winner.

Biodiesel is not quite as perfect as it might first appear, however. Made from either waste vegetable oils and fats, or from specifically grown crops, it does dramatically reduce the amount of oil, not to mention carbon, sulphur and crude oil residue, that is emitted or has to be disposed of. But, safer than petroleum diesel as it is, it can still cause some damage to water and wildlife. Ensuring minimum spillage is therefore always important.

Funding was important as the costs of the fuels had to be subsidised to give a fair comparison between biodiesel and petroleum, or red, diesel.

The outcome was that the performance of boats was not affected by using biodiesel. Engines needed no conversion work to use it. There were some problems with storage of the fuel in the winter months when it tended to freeze because of the wax it contained, but it seemed that there were some fairly simple and effective solutions to that in the use of special tanks. Despite biodiesel proving more expensive, it was generally agreed that it had potential for the future. Its use was adopted in what was described at that stage as an 'ad hoc' manner. There was a problem in that the only way to make the fuel more cost effective, and comparable, was through a subsidy, which was complicated to administer.

There was another issue with biodiesel: its lack of supply. This had proved to be a sticking point with boatyards who, commendably, had tried to use it before the tests. It was Norfolk who would lead the way to solve that issue. Global Commodities UK opened in the county, the country's sole purpose-built biodiesel production plant.

Electricity was the other ecology-friendly fuel worth exploring; it had positive and negative factors. On the plus side, electric boats are quiet, emit no exhaust and cause little wake. They therefore have little impact on wildlife, and create minimum erosion of riverbanks. So far, so good. On the minus side, batteries are heavy, and contain lots of metal components.

Put to the test, though, it was difficult to find fault with the concept of electric power for boats. Not only was it viable in new boats, but conventional boats could be converted. A great test of this, especially for the Broads, was the conversion to electric motor of the 26-foot traditional wherry *White Moth*. Taking out her old diesel engine and replacing it with an 8.5-watt motor proved successful both in terms of power and manoeuvrability.

The programme of tests carried out by the authority and boatyards came to an end in 2008. What had been learned was that biodiesel was a potentially important fuel for the future. Availability could be a problem, and that might mean the co-operation of interested parties in a way not examined before. Could it be that farmers would now need to grow special crops in order to make fuel for the boats that cruised waterways which they too had a responsibility to protect?

As to electricity, it was a clean and viable power source, but boats would need places to 'charge up'. The Broads Authority was swift to move on not only providing more charging points, but also to facilitate grants for converting boats to electric power.

In their 2011 report on sustainable tourism, the Broads Authority was able to look back on the progress made since 2005. It was then that they had formed a vision for the Broads. Much of that vision had come to be. Several Broads species had grown in number, or established themselves in new locations. Wildlife in general could be considered more abundant and some species, including swallowtail butterflies, kingfishers and otters were demonstrably more visible. There had been significant improvements to moorings, areas of wetland had been brought into conservation, new 'eco-boat' designs were in hand and there had been restoration work carried out at important heritage sights. There had been progress in conserving the Broads, and although boat numbers had levelled out, there were new craft and there had been a couple of good trading years. The important point about all of this, and indeed several other achievements of the period, is that they involved *partnerships*. The much-discussed concept of people working together for the future of the Broads appeared to be succeeding.

Certainly the Broads Authority had been busy. In among the myriad of programmes and projects with which they were involved there had, by 2009, been another Act of Parliament to build on the original 1988 Norfolk and Suffolk Broads Act. The Broads Authority had promoted the new Act in 2006 with the main aim of introducing better safety controls on the Broads. They were successful. When the Broads Authority Act gained the royal assent in 2009 it included provisions to empower the authority in several areas, including the introduction of hire-boat licensing and compulsory third-party insurance. It also introduced controls on waterskiing and wakeboarding.

These activities in particular demonstrated that what people wanted to do in the area was changing and developing, as it always had. Certainly the traditional interests of sailing, birdwatching and angling still held their appeal; given the more environmentally friendly consumer of the twenty-first century, they were possibly growing. There were by now several organised trips to areas of interest, which allowed viewing with minimum danger to the environment. Walking and cycling were popular. Camping and caravanning now accounted for over 40 per cent of the visitors' accommodation. The visitors were coming mainly from the South East, and often came in families, although couples were an important sector.

Research at the time indicated that people liked the Broads. They wanted to see the area 'preserved' rather than developed. Visitors didn't seem to be particularly aware of the Broads' position regarding the family of national parks, but they did feel that the area was well managed and 'clean and tidy'.

In overall terms there were, as ever, the interests of all parties to consider when it came to using the knowledge that was being acquired about the Broads in the first decade of the twenty-first century. In the area itself there was plainly more cohesion in the Broads' management and care. Outside Norfolk, though, did people have a real view of the Broads?

Businesses had seen some growth in recent times but they had also invested, and now they wanted a return. That meant visitors were needed. It also meant that new visitors were needed because changing demographics meant that the future could not be built on repeat business. The loyalty of regular Broads visitors could not be taken for granted.

Hitherto, when the concept of marketing had come into view on the Broads horizon it had, the Broads Authority aside, been directly connected to the boat hire and holiday companies. Even when the railway companies, as they had in the 1930s, advertised 'THE BROADS', they had done so to promote their brand.

When a new brand arrived, it would be 'the Broads'.

Broads Tourism had been established in 2004, with its roots in the Broads Boating Holidays Project and fuelled by the realisation that, over and above the outstanding work being done in so many ways, there was now a need to create a 'forum' or united effort to promote tourism on the Broads. The pressures of competition from a vast range of other holiday activities, combined with the need to attract *new* visitors to the Broads, meant that it was time to both focus on a campaign for tourism and find the common ground between the numerous businesses in Norfolk, all of whom would benefit from more visitors.

When the concept was put to them, local business responded positively. Boatyards, pubs, hotels, as well as landowners and councils joined. Conservation groups and the Broads Authority were engaged. Things began to happen quickly. Soon, Broads Tourism had built a database of companies to speed up communications. Campaigning had started with initiatives on improving litter removal and toilet facilities. Proving the point that this was an inclusive and forward-thinking organisation, there were applications for funding made, including one for work with the Green Tourism Scheme.

In communications terms, the tourism strategy was drafted, a 'Visit the Broads' website conceived and, by 2005, at the International Boat Show, the first 'Broads brochure' was launched.

It was Broads Tourism who, with their continued enthusiasm for a unified voice for Broadland, developed the Broads brand that appeared in 2010. With it came the brand's line: 'The Broads. Britain's magical waterland.' The brand has been developed into a regular brochure and the informative website www.enjoythebroads. com, which carries details of responsible leisure and entertainment facilities on the Broads.

It has been successful in bringing visitors to the Broads, but Broads Tourism has also demonstrated and delivered the integration of effort and communication that had long been sought. By definition that could not have been achieved in isolation and it's the active involvement of the Broads Authority, as well as numerous local businesses, that has characterised the decade, making the Broads an ever better destination.

At the same time, another player was about to add weight to the campaign to sell holidays on the Norfolk Broads. Far from inactive across the media in general, the Hoseasons brand had been absent from TV advertising since 2007.

In 2010, the company had been acquired by Wyndham Worldwide. The international holiday accommodation business bought it from the private equity group who owned it after James Hoseason had retired.

James Hoseason, or 'Jimmy' as he was known to so many, had already passed away. He'd been unwell for some months when he died at the Norfolk and Norwich University Hospital in November 2009.

Implementing a strategy that would have doubtless obtained 'Jimmy's' approval, the new owners planned a return to TV with a campaign to break on Boxing Day. The 2011 advertising and marketing strategy was based on an integrated approach. The TV commercial would appear on ITV, Channels 4 and 5, as well as digital channels. Whole-page advertisements in the national Sunday press colour supplements would run throughout January, while the TV campaign continued into February.

It wasn't the first time that the brand had used celebrity endorsement, but now they introduced a new face. Totally in keeping with the times and immediately recognisable from television, and the West End run of *Legally Blonde*, it was Denise van Outen who starred in the new commercial. This was a different Hoseasons from the company who had first used television advertising decades earlier. Miss van Outen was seen experiencing all sorts of Hoseasons holidays, and places to stay – 'like this, or this,' before she said, '*even* this' when it came to mentioning the Broads. The sheer size of the campaign, and the brand, albeit under new ownership, would be good for the Broads, which remained an essential part of the company's portfolio of holiday offerings. But it was interesting to see how much the business had developed, and how the Broads were now but a part of it. Similar in so many ways to earlier strategies, this campaign needed to address the fact that things had changed. Now it was brand before destination, because there were lots of destinations.

The Hoseasons campaign was running, along with those of many other national holiday companies, when the Broads Authority launched their very specifically Norfolk 'Broads Plan 2011'.

Dr J. S. Johnson, in the chairman's foreword to the document, made it clear that this was a plan not just for the Broads Authority, but for the Broads. Some of the content of the plan has already been alluded to, but it is timely to look in more detail at it now. The three big themes of the plan were given as planning for the long-term future of the Broads in response to climate change and sea-level rise; working in partnership on the sustainable management of the Broads; and encouraging the sustainable use and enjoyment of the Broads.

These, then, were the key objectives. The plan developed these themes in considerable detail, in a document of considerable scope. It's interesting to compare it with the 1948 *Anchors Aweigh!*, which contained a message from the Broads Protection Society. In it the society had said that, every year, more and more people visited Broadland to discover what a 'restful, healthy, interesting, instructive and enjoyable holiday' could be obtained there. However, it cautioned, 'steadily nature is causing this once wide three-pronged estuary to diminish and the numbers and sizes of Broads are slowly shrinking'.

Given the society's purpose to 'extend, restore and preserve the Broadland Area for present and future generations of holidaymakers as well as to safeguard the rights of the Public in such matters as navigation, moorings and the like', the suggestion, or request, had been for all holidaymakers to join by paying 2s 6d.

What had changed in the fifty-three years between the two publications? At face value, very little. Both are concerned with preserving the Broads for 'now' and 'the future'. There is an element of 'partnership' working in the 1948 message, although it is embryonic.

There had been a discernible shift, though. By 2011, the problems of climate change and sea level feature prominently. In 1948, 'nature' was certainly seen as the culprit, enemy even, in the struggle to protect the Broads. Not even aware that the Broads are man-made, the writer of the 1948 message made no reference to man causing the problems. In the years between the two documents man, and 'holidaymaking on a boat man', would become the prime suspect in the crimes of erosion and contamination. By the 2011 report, not only had man's 'guilt' been put into perspective but awareness of climate change had brought nature back into the witness box. Man's contribution to climate change does not, of course, clear him of all charges. Certainly his endeavours to work together in partnership, and to encourage sustainable enjoyment of the Broads, had begun to ameliorate his role in the matter, but not by enough to settle the score.

Ironically, the other threat looming was sea-level rise, the same problem that faced the peat diggings of 800 years earlier.

Alongside the Broads Plan for 2011–2015, the Broads Authority had also produced a strategy document for sustainable tourism for the same period. This too was comprehensive and detailed. Having examined the condition of the area, the strategy document set out to define the actions needed. What had become clear was that, while the Broads Authority would continue to play an important role, the central responsibility for implementing the strategy should be placed with Broads Tourism.

The quest for the Broads to be managed by a central body, which had been so often expressed and debated, was in place in the form of the Broads Authority, but so too was the less tangible but equally demonstrable cohesion that had been the other great objective, and the efforts of everybody concerned were plainly much more focused on the protection and condition of the Broads. The Norfolk Broads in the first decade of the twenty-first century was a place where recreation and conservation now worked together in a range of innovative and positive ways.

In 2009, the Broads Authority had, for instance, applied for and won some half a million Euros in funding from the European Regional Development Fund to promote tourism with a 'green focus'. A three-year project, this was part of STEP (Sustainable Tourism in Estuary Parks) and involved working in partnership with parks in the Netherlands and Belgium. It was from this experience that Broads Tourism would work with local commerce to continue to promote the Broads region as a whole, and launch the enjoythebroads.com website.

Also in 2009, the Broads Authority appointed a member of their staff to work with what would become the Green Boat and Tourism Show. This venture had started life in the 1990s under the title 'A Silent Sensation'. Organised by the Broads Society, its aim was to increase awareness of electric boats. It was a relatively small, quite informal event staged near South Walsham Broad in the garden of a Broads Society member. By 2006, it had become the 'The Broads Green Boat Show' and was by then, assisted by a grant from Leader+ and the Sustainable Development Fund, able to do more to promote sustainable ideas to a wider public. A significant part of its agenda was the conversion of existing boats, and through its efforts some twenty craft were duly switched to electric power. By now the show had moved to Salhouse Broad and was regularly attended by a growing number of local businesses.

Among them was Norfolk Broads Direct, a company committed to sustainable ideology. When they exhibited at the 2011 show, they did so having scored a valuable point for themselves and the Broads. The Green Boat Mark had been launched as a means of recognising sustainable practice, and it was Wroxham-based Norfolk Broads Direct who had become the first fleet in the country to be awarded the accreditation.

Mandatory in meeting the mark were the provision of phosphate-free cleaners and water management. Norfolk Broads Direct had also been working on heating the water on some of its fleet as a by-product of the engine cooling system. It was a serious signal to the world that Norfolk meant what it said.

The year 2012 saw the event's name changed again to the 'Green Boat and Tourism Show', to represent more accurately and comprehensively what it was about. From its relatively humble beginnings, this event had become the UK's sole boat show to promote actively the new technologies, deliver a message of sustainable boating as a truly valid option within tourism and showcase companies who were positively engaged with a 'green' agenda for the Broads.

The next change in its history was the timing. Previously held in September, 'The Green Boat and Tourism Show' now moved to May. There was a very good reason. It would now become the finale to another major event in the widening canvas of activity on the Broads.

The first Broads Outdoor Festival had been organised by the Broads Authority. With links to the world-famous Norfolk and Norwich Festival and some funding from STEP, the show was aimed at meeting two key objectives. Firstly, it would promote Broads Tourism in the slower period between Easter and Whitsun. Secondly, it could deliver the message that the Broads had so much to offer as well as boating. Inspired by the Broads Authority, it was another clear demonstration of businesses working together. Over sixty events and activities were combined into a festival that would grow and develop into an annual event.

By 2013, with continued organisation from the Broads Authority and Broads Tourism, plus support from media group Archant, and Hoseasons, the festival had become hugely popular. Celebrating history in a Victorian steam launch, or embracing the future in a solar-powered boat, visitors could learn about wind pumps and wildlife, go canoeing, birdwatching or cycling. It was, and is, the all-embracing picture of what makes the Norfolk Broads magical.

Magical was a word that still had a resonance in Broadland. The festival was, it was said, a great opportunity to discover Britain's Magical Waterland. This phrase, used by Dr Stephen Johnson, chairman of the Broads Authority, in his welcome to the official 'programme' and on promotional material, had been coined in 2010 as part of a branding project put together by the Broads Authority and Broads Tourism. The aims were completely in keeping with the widely stated strategic objectives. There would be a logo and images, together with key messages, put together in a 'toolkit' for boat-hire firms, hotels and other local businesses to have a united and consistent message for the Broads.

'Britain's Magical Waterland' as the slogan to rebrand the Norfolk Broads did not, however, meet with unified approval. Fairly or unfairly, the reaction to the new branding was vociferous. Defended by the Norfolk Tourism Forum as brave and necessary in the fight to gain still-needed visitors to the area, and to position the region as a key destination, the public reaction in Norfolk was in some cases hostile. There was anger that, seemingly, no local residents had been consulted about the idea, and there were feelings that it was an unnecessary move. People asked why money had been spent on a 'brand' when the real issue was fact that Norfolk was hard to get to; money and effort would be better spent, it was said, on lobbying for, and improving, transport links to the county. The widening of the A11, the main road into Norfolk from the south, was inevitably raised as it had been a long-running concern.

Like so many changes and developments in branding, across all markets and products, the new identity had, for the moment at least, divided opinion.

Concerted, greener, rebranded, whatever efforts were being put into 'Britain's Magical Waterland' were apparently having results. The Scarborough Tourism Economic Activity Monitor (STEAM) is a highly respected business model for calculating the value of tourism and when it released figures for 2011 it showed that visitors to the Broads had spent £469 million that year, compared to £437 million in 2010. A count of 7.4 million visitors in 2011 represented a 4.2 per cent increase over 2010 and they'd delivered a 2 per cent increase in spending. Jobs in Broads tourism had increased too.

This, of course, had been achieved in a difficult economic climate, and the Broads Authority and Broads Tourism were quick, and justified, in pointing out that, in such times, the results were tribute to the hard work of everybody concerned. Broads Tourism, representing businesses and the Broads Authority, had pulled together to identify the areas that needed addressing and now commerce, environment and visitors were all benefiting.

As this story of the Broads approaches the present day, it's timely to look at what is happening in this most recent chapter, the twenty-first century's second decade.

It's a sad point to make, but the country was shocked in 2012 by a crime on the Broads. Criminal activity is not unheard of on the Broads, but by and large it is a peaceful area. Bad behaviour on boats is as old as boating itself, and references to loud antics and drinking in the 1920s and 1930s especially are to be found in fact and fiction. In 2011, Broads police had issued quite clear statements about behaviour over the spring bank holiday weekend. There had been several incidents of drunkenness in Wroxham and Horning. The stance taken by the police was that alcohol and water are a dangerous combination. Safety was paramount, and not helped by people lighting barbecues next to fuel tanks for instance. It was also pointed out that, given various collisions, it was an offence to be at the helm of a boat while under the influence of alcohol and drugs. Sizeable fines could be levied.

As serious as this level of, relatively rare, behaviour was, it paled into insignificance against the events of 1 September 2012. On that morning, police were called to Salhouse Broad. A Broads Authority Ranger had spotted a moored boat some days earlier and, returning from patrol that September morning, thought it best to investigate. He knocked on the side of the boat and discovered a thirteen-year-old girl aboard, and alone.

The young girl explained that she, together with her mother and her mother's partner, had come for a holiday, arriving on 25 August. John Didier was a forty-one-year-old NHS worker. His partner, forty-nine-year-old Annette Creegan, was a hospice nurse. They knew the Broads, having spent holidays there before, and when they took out their boat from Horning they were well prepared and stocked with provisions.

When the girl had woken up on the morning after they'd arrived, her mother was nowhere to be found. John Didier told her that she'd 'left'. With no mobile phone and unable to leave the boat, the girl stayed with Didier for the next few days. Six days later the girl had gone to bed as normal, but when she woke up that morning there was no sign of Didier either.

A search was launched. They found Annette Creegan's naked body, strangled and held down by weights, in the River Bure. Didier's body was not far away. It appeared he had drowned himself by jumping overboard, having first bound himself to some dumb-bells. The inquest revealed that this was the case, the dumb-bells on his feet weighing some 17.5 kg each and those on his hands 15 kg each.

Originally from Ohio, USA, John Didier worked in IT for the NHS. Despite his being unemployed at the time of their holiday, investigations showed that there appeared to be no particular tensions between the couple. Annette's daughter had heard no arguments on the boat. With no reason to assume that John had any mental health issues, there seemed no motive for what appeared to be a carefully premeditated crime.

Annette Creegan had been strangled, and her body, weighted and cable-tied, had been dropped into the river. There was no evidence that anybody else was involved. The stark truth was that John Didier had equipped himself with the weights and prepared for the murder. He killed Annette and then spent almost a week on board the Broads cruiser with her daughter before killing himself, leaving the girl alone.

Recording a verdict that Ms Creegan had died as the result of unlawful killing, and that John Didier had committed suicide, the Norfolk coroner William Armstrong offered his condolences to both families. He added what many people thought when he said, 'What a grotesque irony that this happened in the idyllic setting of the Norfolk Broads – what a contrast between the calm serenity of the waters and this dreadful tragedy.'

The tragedy would take on another irony when, in 2013, a national survey was commissioned for the Institute of Economics and Peace. It showed that the UK had seen a 'substantial and sustained' fall in violent crime over the past decade. Three Rivers in Hertfordshire, South Cambridgeshire, East Dorset and Maldon in Essex were seen as very peaceful places. Above them all, and rated as the most peaceful area at local authority level in the UK, was one place: Broadland.

Rare tragedies aside, the Broads are a place of beauty and calm. Bustling at times perhaps, but still a tranquil area. It was the appeal that had brought stars of the entertainment world to relax there in bygone decades and it remains as strong as ever. Where once George Formby had been sighted, now movie fans spotted Hollywood superstars such as Mila Kunis and Ashton Kutcher, who stayed on a Broads boat in 2013. She was filming nearby, and he hired a boat to be able to join her. Almost inevitably, the press coverage referred to their heading for the 'sleepy' Norfolk Broads.

More than once in this story, the Broads have been identified as 'sleepy'. Many times it's been with the blessing of those who work there, to encourage visitors and promote the area's beauty. Often, though, it's been a less-than-positive comment from those who choose to see Norfolk as somewhere out of step and behind the times. As is often the case with Norfolk, those who live there know that the joke is on the detractors. 'Sleepy' it might be when it comes to being somewhere to relax, but holidaymakers go there because for decades the Broads have been promoted by some of the most innovative, not to say groundbreaking, marketing. Boatbuilding in Norfolk has been world-class, with techniques and materials being developed to match cutting-edge design. The area has been protected and managed by some of the most skilful, dedicated and resourceful people implementing the most modern of strategies. Indeed, the amount of effort put in to managing the Broads and in to their protection, it could be argued, puts the area ahead of the game in comparison with other, perhaps sometimes more visible, causes.

Recent developments include more evidence of the modernity of thinking. An 'app' has been introduced to give visitors access to an interactive map of the Broads. Using 3G and Wi-Fi, the app lets people find attractions and moorings. Created by norfolkbroads. com, the technology delivers huge amounts of information on where to go and what to see, as well as specific details of, for example, pet- and wheelchair-friendly locations.

Commerce has been innovative, too. Arguably driven to some extent by necessity, farmers have diversified into holiday accommodation, farm shops and 'pick your own' fruit fields as well as 'Farm Parks'. Cafés, pubs and restaurants have changed the food offered to match current tastes. And of course, on board the Broads boats there are more technology-driven entertainment options. A plasma-screen television might not be in the tradition of the Coot Club, but it is in the spirit of giving the customers what they want.

The attractive sleepiness of the Norfolk Broads belies, and yet endorses, the enterprise of the area's people.

8

A Look Back and a Look Forward

It has been a long voyage from the prehistory of Norfolk's windswept landscape, through invasions and occupations, agricultural development, the discovery of the Broads as a place of recreation and on through the growth of tourism to the twenty-first century. The sociological changes represent a seismic shift. When the Normans invaded Britain in 1066, the country's population, it has been estimated, was around 2 million people. Today over 7 million visit the Broads each year.

By the sixteenth century, Norwich was the second-largest city in England. Despite losing a third of its population in the great plagues, the city was riding on the prosperity of the agricultural and textile business of the county. The Broads were simply stretches of water, with no significant purpose and forgotten origins.

As the importance of agriculture gave way to the Industrial Revolution, the county's fortunes wavered. The great factories and mills had little impact on the Norfolk skyline. They dominated the North and shifted the fulcrum of commercial wealth away from the agricultural lands of East Anglia.

In the meantime, the marsh men and the reed cutters, the wherry crews and the boatbuilders, carved out their livelihoods from the landscape that itself had been excavated in the production of fuel. By the time coal was the nation's prime source of energy, the steam engine was powering the great expansion of the railway boom. Suddenly Norfolk was, despite diminished economic importance, more accessible than ever.

Work in the new industrial age was comparatively lucrative, but demanding. Recreation was becoming a necessity; it could be afforded, and people could travel to find it.

It was the emerging prosperity of what would become the industrial working class that would lead to the concept of holidays and tourism. When it arrived, the Broads were ready. By the late nineteenth century, John Loynes and others were shaping the nascent Broads boating holiday industry. Artists, writers and early photographers have left us a snapshot of this world, capturing the Broads on a tipping point that would set in motion the great balancing act that has characterised their existence ever since. Even then, the newfound prosperity from visitors was beginning to be offset against the loss of environment and identity caused by their arrival.

But they continued to arrive; and they came not just from the factories and mills but from the equally rapidly growing banks and finance houses, shops and insurance offices. Clerks and salesmen also needed time away from the pace of working life in the new century. One of them was Harry Blake. Being on holiday did not remove his commercial zeal. Unknowingly, the world was just a heartbeat away from war, sequestered in Edwardian calm, when he saw the opportunity for a more organised approach to selling Broads holidays. His starting an agency in 1908 was arguably the first time someone put a firmer hand on the tiller.

Britain, let alone the Broads, was never the same again after the First World War. In the two brief decades of peace before the next great conflict, the social and economic map of the country was redrawn. The 1930s saw times of terrible depression and yet it was a time, perhaps in reaction to the reality, in which the Broads emerged in art, literature and commercial history as a place of happy holidays and waterborne fun. This was the era of the new power cruisers, white-flannelled young blades playing their gramophones on board, their image of the perfect Broads holiday trapped forever in the stylish graphics of the railway posters of the period. Once again, an idyll was shattered by war.

Deflected by, and diversified into, war effort, the Norfolk Broads emerged from the Second World War in a mess of neglected boats, redundant blockades and dangerous obstacles in the shape of sunken craft, including some of its legendary wherries. As the clouds lifted, heaving to alongside Blakes was another name: Hoseason. With an idea born of wartime logistics, Wally Hoseason steered his business towards boating holidays before his son James took it out into midstream and set sail for the future. By the 1950s, these two great names would dominate the rapidly expanding Broads holiday industry, and the great British public would fuel its growth with an unprecedented enthusiasm.

It was then, with all eyes set on the future, that the past came zooming back into focus. The work of Dr Joyce Lambert not only questioned the existing knowledge but delivered new proof as to how the Broads had come into being in the first place. It was established that they were man-made. The problem now emerging was that it was man who was damaging them.

All of the weights could now be put into the scales and balanced. Tourism meant work and prosperity. Increased boat traffic, on the other hand, was seen as damaging the Broads. The post-war public wanted recreation, and deserved it. But at what cost to the environment? Marketing, embraced by many, was putting the Norfolk Broads on the map. But, derided by others, it was seen as the area losing its way. Pumping up consumer awareness was fine, until those consumers pumped out their boat's tanks into the Broads. Slowly, as the waters – metaphorically for the moment – cleared, it became apparent that to focus on tourism as the sole cause of environmental problems was a dangerous mistake. Agriculture, the water companies, phosphates and sewage were contributory factors too, not to mention wildlife itself, and in the light of what boat operators were doing to engender better practice, these were perhaps bigger issues than tourism. It was as if the Broads needed protecting against themselves.

It's little wonder that the constant strain of argument emerging from this time was that of the need for more cohesion between all of those involved with the Broads and the need for a body to manage them. Recreation and conservation would be bound together in legislation as years of proposals, discussions, Bills and Acts of Parliament finally resulted in the Broads Authority. As ever, Norfolk had stood alone, defining itself as different, declining direction from those 'outside' who didn't understand the area, and as a result creating, in the Broads Authority, an organisation that would not only break moulds but be an example to the world.

Riding out the competition from the newly popular overseas holidays of the 1960s and 1970s, the Broads holiday industry forged ahead. With some perceived brand differences, but in truth with one common aim, Blakes and Hoseasons sold more and more holidays on the Broads, but they did more. They developed, beyond the most optimistic imaginings of the pre-war advertising fraternity, an image and an awareness of the Broads. If people didn't buy a holiday there this year, they might the next because now they knew about the Broads. They also delivered more of the much-sought-after cohesion, pulling their weight with improvements to contribute to conservation.

With them were the farmers and water companies, the councils and the pressure groups, the small independent boatyards, the charities and trusts, the public and the politicians, as all now seemed to be far more aware of the problems facing Broadland. Interests may still have differed, and not every issue was met with unanimity, but there was, plainly, a different and new attitude towards the Norfolk Broads.

Just like the landscape, language changes all the time. On a whimsical level it's entertaining to compare the tone and style of the brochures and advertisements from decades past with today's less 'flowery' style. More profoundly, language has to develop to embrace new ideas. Much earlier in this book there are some dictionary definitions from the nineteenth century and later, showing how the meaning of a Broad was modified over time.

In the twenty-first century another word has been extended and redefined; it's a vital concept. Sustainability.

As late as 1985, dictionaries contained definitions of 'sustain' that understandably referred to 'holding up' or 'supporting'. There was no mention of 'sustainability' in the sense that we know now. The Industrial Revolution, which has already played a role in this history, replaced the need for the fuels such as peat, dug out of Norfolk. It was the era when the fossil fuels, primarily coal, were mined and used in ever growing quantities to feed the engines of progress. It was well into the twentieth century before what would become known as 'environmental movements' began to realise, and point out, that what man was burning today would have an impact on the environment tomorrow. It was a worldwide problem. There were other worries about the future too. Aside from the damage we were causing the planet, we were using up our resources. Our fuels were not only potentially dangerous, they were also finite. The energy crises of the mid-1970s brought into sharp focus the fact that, across the globe, mankind was dependent on energy resources that were not renewable.

By 1987, there was a working definition for not just the concept of sustainability but the more practical implication of sustainable development. The Brundtland Commission, established by the United Nations, declared in the March of that year that 'sustainable development is development that meets the needs of the present without compromising the ability of future generations to meet their own needs'.

It could have been written with the Norfolk Broads in mind. It was echoed precisely by the Broads Authority in their plans, particularly the 2011–2015 'Strategy and Action Plan for Sustainable Tourism in the Broads'.

The title itself of the 2011 plan speaks volumes for the progress made since the days of the early National Park debates. Now there was a managing body, and a strategy; what's more, the concepts of sustainability and tourism were in the same plan.

At the time of this book being written, the 'Plan for Sustainable Tourism' is still 'in hand'. 2015 is one year in the future. Progress is made every day, and in many ways, in terms of both commercial activity and conservation on the Broads. In bringing the story up to date it's important to take a snapshot of some of the current activities and developments in the region.

Innovation still abounds. The recently established Norfolk and Suffolk Broads Charitable Trust has created an initiative to encourage businesses to fund improvement projects through a scheme called 'Love the Broads'. The development officer leading the project will work with conservation groups as well, further evidencing the greater cohesion of the new century. Among the myriad of their activities, the Broads Authority have created an integrated access strategy, aimed at improving the pathways and links between moorings and villages. Involving numerous organisations, the strategy will enhance the Broads experience for those on land-based holidays as well as visiting boaters. The project is directly connected, in its early stages, to restoration work at that most historic of Broads locations, St Benet's Abbey.

In the summer of 2013, a local media campaign sought people's views on 'what Norfolk means to you'. The Norfolk Broads figured highly in the responses.

In July 2013, the last three remaining wherry yachts sailed at Ranworth. It was the first time that the three craft had sailed together in eighty years. *Norada*, *White Moth* and the 1909-built *Olive* were a majestic sight. Testament to the work of the Wherry Yacht Charter Charitable Trust, Heritage Lottery Fund input and, among others, Defra's Rural Development Programme for England, these stately survivors will sail into the future. *Hathor*, another wherry yacht, will, it's hoped, join them. It will take money to maintain the four craft. The trust is exploring all the options, including corporate hire and unusual holidays on skippered craft. It has an eerie resonance with the way in which the original wherry skippers faced the need to change.

It's as if the Broads are looking to the future, but never forgetting to take a look over their shoulder at the past. Once again, resourcefulness and adaptability, resilience and endeavour, will be the hallmarks of the Broads and their people. Always learning from and celebrating the past, but always creating a better future.

The Broads Authority, the trusts, the media and the hundreds of businesses that comprise the Broads are now working together. So too are two of the names that, along with the authority, have recurred time and again in this history of the Broads. Blakes and Hoseasons are now within the same company. The two brands operate within the Wyndham organisation as part of the Hoseason Group. Competitors for so long, these now sister brands continue to provide holidays for millions of people, in the great tradition of the Broads.

Cared for, the Broads will carry their traditions long into the future.

Bibliography

In writing this book I've drawn on the huge amount of material available concerning the Norfolk Broads. Much of it, of course, is now online, and I have carried out extensive research through websites and Internet archives.

I have also had the opportunity of, and pleasure in, talking with people who are actively involved with the Norfolk Broads. Once again I express my gratitude in particular to the following:

Simon Altham, Katie Hanger, Geri Colt, Sara West, Rebecca Harris and Mark Chambers at Hoseasons.
Hilary Franzen and Bruce Hanson at the Broads Authority.
Colin and Lesley Dye at Silvermarine in Brundall.
Sue Bell and Bryan Cadamy, from Summercraft in Hoveton.
Barbara Greasley and her team at Broads Tours in Wroxham.

Among the vast amount of literature I studied for the book, I would make special mention of the following:

The Vocabulary of East Anglia, Robert Forby (J. B. Nichols & Son, 1830)
The Handbook to the Rivers and Broads of Norfolk and Suffolk, G. Christopher Davies (Jarrolds, 1882)

The Land of the Broads, Ernest Suffling (Benjamin Perry, 1892)

Highways & Byways in East Anglia, W. A. Dutt (Macmillan & Co., 1901)

Revisiting the works of Arthur Ransome has been a pleasure, in particular, *Coot Club* (Jonathan Cape, 1934)

The Future of Broadland (University of East Anglia, 1977)

A Century of Broadland Cruising, Charles Goodey (J. Loynes & Sons Ltd, 1978)

'Boat-Hire Holidays on The Norfolk Broads' (A report published by The Norfolk & Suffolk Broads Yacht Owners Association, Wroxham, and The Broadland Owners Association, Oulton Broad, 1979)

The Battle for The Broads, Martin Ewans (Terence Dalton Ltd, 1992)

'Broads Plan' (The Broads Authority, 2011)

'Sustainable Tourism in The Broads' (The Broads Authority, 2011)

About the Author

Pete Goodrum is a Norwich man. He has had a successful career in advertising agencies, working on national and international campaigns, and now works as a freelance advertising writer and consultant.

Pete is also a successful author. His book *Norwich in the 1950s*, published by Amberley, topped the local bestseller charts for almost three months in 2012, and his sequel *Norwich in the 1960s*, also published by Amberley, was a bestseller in 2013.

He makes frequent appearances on BBC local radio, covering topics ranging from advertising to music and social trends. A regular reader at live poetry sessions, and actively involved in the media, Pete has a real passion for the history of Norwich and Norfolk.

He lives in the centre of the city with his wife, Sue.

Also available from Amberley Publishing

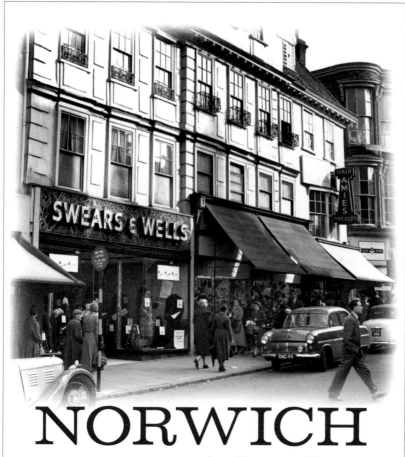

NORWICH
in the 1950s
Ten Years that Changed a City

PETE GOODRUM

Available from all good bookshops or to order direct
Please call **01453-847-800**
www.amberleybooks.com

Also available from Amberley Publishing

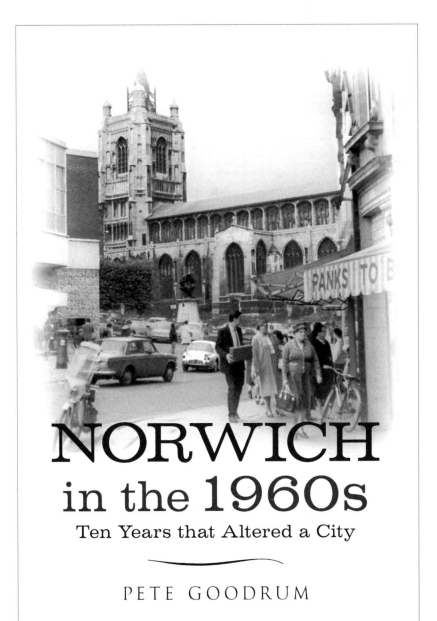

NORWICH
in the 1960s
Ten Years that Altered a City

PETE GOODRUM

Available from all good bookshops or to order direct
Please call **01453–847–800**
www.amberleybooks.com

Index